A MOMENT FOR MYSTERY

Have you heard Jesus say, "*You are the light of the world!*"? Have you heard him say it to you? Really heard it? Do you really believe it?

He did say it. Word for word. To all of us (*Matthew* 5:14). But we may have heard it as if he were speaking on ground level. On the level of metaphor; not mystery.

If that is the way we heard it, we have never heard it. And if we have never heard it, the Gospel has not been preached to us. If we are not *immersed in mystery*, we are not immersed in Christ. We are only dabbling our feet in Christianity.

Imagine Jesus Christ standing before you. Looking into your eyes and saying, "*You are the light of the world*! I who am the Light of Life am sharing my Life with you. Now my Light is your Light. You are a mystery of light shining in the darkness. Let your light shine! Give glory to your Father in heaven!"

What does that do to you? How can you ever be the same?

God has given us *enlightenment*. And promised us more. To all who read his words he promises enlightenment. God promises. To everyone who reads. How can we stay away from a guaranteed source of mystical enlightenment? From a channel of light that is certified to deliver? Certified by Jesus Christ himself, "God from God, Light from Light, true God from true God." How could anyone, offered the gift of divine enlightenment by Jesus himself, turn away from being a *disciple*?[1]

If we turn away, the *Liturgy of the Word* calls us back. In every Mass. The Church's instructions on liturgy tell us:

> The liturgy of the word must be celebrated in such a way as to *promote meditation*…. in which the Word of God is taken into the heart by the fostering of the Holy Spirit and response to it is prepared by prayer."[2]

Reflection on Scripture is *discipleship*. It is accepting the gift of Light.

These reflections "zoom in" on whatever there is in the lectionary readings that speaks to the theme of *discipleship*, "*metanoia*," the "complete makeover" of mind and heart and direction that is the purpose and focus of Lent. Read to be challenged.

If we read and reflect on the word of God we will experience the *enlightenment* promised to us at Baptism. The Church believes that:

> In the sacred books the Father who is in heaven *meets his children* with great love and *speaks with them*. And the force and power in the word of God is so great that it remains the support and energy of the Church.[3]

These reflections simply aim to help us listen to the voice of God.

---

[1]To be a *disciple* it is not enough to "follow Jesus." The word "disciple" means "student." Those Jesus called in the Gospels to be "disciples" he called aside for special instruction (*Mark* 4:34).
[2]*General Instruction on the Roman Missal*, 2000, no. 56; *Documents of Vatican II: The Church*, no. 11.
[3]Vatican II, "Liturgy," no. 33.

FEBRUARY 6, 2011
We Are the Light of the World

INVENTORY

Is anything wrong with our society? Closer to home, is there anything wrong in your family life? Work situation? Social life? Do you ever blame God for any it?

INPUT

The *Entrance Antiphon* calls us to "worship the Lord.... bow down in the presence of our maker." We "bow down" before him in adoration because he is awesome, all powerful, the one who gave and is giving us right now our very existence. For this we owe him respect and trusting obedience: "He is the Lord our God."

The *Opening Prayer(s)* builds on this: "Father, watch over your family... all our hope is in you." God, as the Giver of existence, is all present. He is in all things, sustaining them in existence, giving them power to act. So we say, "No thought of ours is left unguarded, no tear unheeded, no joy unnoticed." We say he has assumed responsibility for our well-being. So why are things such a mess?

The *Communion* prayer ends with a surprise: "Help *us* to bring your salvation and joy to all the world." God is making it *our* responsibility to straighten things out on earth. That changes the meaning of "all our hope is in you." Now it means we are trusting in him to *help us do* what needs to be done. We are the world's hope, and our hope is in what God empowers us to do.

The prayers point to the way God does it through the Mass. His Body and Blood "give us nourishment" and "make us one," united in faith, mutual support, and action. But there is more. We must not overlook the power in the *Liturgy of the Word.* God nourishes, strengthens, and unites us through his word:

> The Church has always venerated the divine Scriptures *just as she venerates the body of the Lord*, since *from the table of both* the word of God and of the body of Christ she unceasingly receives and offers to the faithful the bread of life, especially in the sacred liturgy.[1]

Now it all comes together: God's answer to the darkness of the world is to put his light in us and send us out to "give light to all in the house," everywhere we are: at home, at work, in social and civic life. Jesus said, "As long as I am in the world, I am the light of the world." But since we are his body, he is in the world as long as we are. He said to his disciples, "*You* are the light of the world." We are sent out "to give light to those who sit in darkness and in the shadow of death, to guide their feet into the way of peace." For this we need to be students of his word.[2]

[1] Vatican II, "Revelation," no. 21.
[2] *John* 9:5; *Matthew* 5:14-15; *Luke* 1:79.

WE NEED TO SHINE

The *Responsorial* (*Psalm* 112) gives the key to all the readings: "*The just are a light in darkness to the upright.*" Those Christians who are "just," who live by what they believe, are a "light in darkness" to anyone who is "upright" enough to be open to truth. Jesus said, "Everyone who belongs to the truth listens to my voice," and "Whoever listens to you listens to me."

Whatever religion people follow, if they are in contact with God, they can communicate with anyone else who knows God. John said, "Whoever knows God listens to us." And if we know God, we will listen to anyone else who does. Light does not reject light. And when believers are unified in light, they are a force to contend with.[1]

Isaiah 58:7-10 puts the emphasis on living the light. It shines through our actions. We Christians are often at fault for not sharing our faith in words. We are embarrassed to show devotion. But our greatest failure is in living out the faith in action.[2]

Isaiah says, "If you remove from your midst oppression, false accusation, and malicious speech...." We may accuse ourselves of these sins on the personal level, if we ourselves take advantage of others, lie, or destroy their reputations. But do we take responsibility for the ways we as a nation oppress and exploit others economically? Do we repeat the accusations against politicians and public figures that are proliferated on the internet and in the media without checking them out? Do we listen to those talk shows that with a thin veneer of humor are nothing but negative humor and hate? Hate divides, and is the work of the devil. Those guided by the Spirit follow the principle St. Ignatius of Loyola enunciated so well:

Every good Christian ought to be more eager to put a good interpretation on a neighbor's statement than to condemn it. Further, if one cannot interpret it favorably, one should ask how the other means it. If that meaning is wrong, one should correct the person with love. And if this is not enough, search out every appropriate means through which, by understanding the statement in a good way, it may be saved.[3]

How much would this practice alone help to heal the divisions between "conservatives" and "liberals" in the Church? Not to mention politics!

In **Matthew 5:13-16** Jesus tells us we are the "light of the world." At the same time he tells us we are the "salt of the earth." In the Bible, salt brings out the taste in food and preserves it. Metaphorically, it is that which keeps human relationships peaceful and makes speech gracious and intelligent.[4]

Jesus says salt is "good for nothing but to be thrown out" when it goes flat. But light is useless when it is invisible, hidden "under a bushel basket." So he says to us who know him, "Let your light shine before others, so that they may see your good works and give glory to your Father in heaven."

This is the answer to the mess the world is in. Christians need to let the light that is in them shine in the darkness. We need to speak out the truth revealed to us. And let it become visible in our actions. Jesus identifies letting the "light shine" with people seeing our "good works." Not to give us credit for them—that doesn't seem to enter his mind—but to "give glory to your Father in heaven." Our "works" should visibly be inspired by ideals so far above ground level, beyond cultural human values, that people will recognize we are empowered "from above." By our Father in heaven.

Letting our light shine doesn't begin in the marketplace, the voting booth, or in the ranks of political protest. It begins at home. In our circle of closest friends. If we don't share the light of our insights and personal experiences of God with those nearest and dearest to us, something fundamental is lacking in our Christian life and ministry.

How many fathers share with their sons and daughters, not what their children should think about God, but what they themselves *feel*? How many children have any clue what their parents' real experience of God is? How many people share this with their friends? With those they date? How many of our neighbors know anything about our religion or what it means to us?

For that matter, how many spouses talk deeply with each other about their experience of God? Or lack of it? (To show one knows what is missing is already to reveal faith and hope). Would it be farfetched to say that a root problem in Christianity is that Christians don't swell the light by *expressing* faith, hope, and love in family life?

And what kind of circle of friends do you have if you are not eager to come together regularly to discuss the Scripture and share your responses to it? If all you have in common is drinking, TV, sports, and small talk—or even large talk that shies away from God—you aren't real friends

to each other. You are just casual acquaintances in the departure gate, whiling away the time until your flight is called.

In **1Corinthians 2:1-5** Paul tells us what Christian communication is. We don't exclude intellectual conversation —no one was more "theological" than Paul—but we aren't really sharing as Christians in the "communion of the Holy Spirit" until we go beyond "the persuasive force of 'wise' arguments" and build each other up with the "convincing power of the Spirit."

Why do we find it so threatening to pray together? To talk about the fruits or failures of our prayer? Don't we have a common God? Don't we share the same Father? Isn't Jesus the Teacher, Friend, and Lover of us all? Weren't we all given the gift of the Spirit who dwells in our hearts? So why do we exclude the Father, Son, and Spirit from our conversation as if they were weird relatives we are ashamed of?

Think of what we don't find it weird to talk about: enslavement to business; the idolatry of sports; the insanity of conformity to the culture; the trivia of style in grooming, dress, and housing; addiction to the latest technology. If this is the level on which we share, this is probably the level on which we live—suffocating under our own bushel basket. Do something about that!

[1]*John* 18:37; *Luke* 10:16; *1John* 4:6
[2]*Matthew* 10:32-33.
[3]*Spiritual Exercises*, no. 22: "Presupposition"; tr. George Ganss, S.J., Loyola Univ. Press, 1992.
[4]*Job* 6:6; *Baruch* 6:27; *Mark* 9:50; *Colossians* 4:6.

INSIGHT

If it is true that "out of the abundance of the heart the mouth speaks" (Matthew 12:34), where does this put you?

INITIATIVE:

Fill your heart with the words of Scripture. Fill your mouth with them too.

FEBRUARY 7, 2011

Genesis 1:1-19; Psalm 104; Mark 6:53-56.

May the Lord be glad in his works!

In every culture parents have had to answer basic questions posed by their children: "Where did I come from?" "Why does it get dark at night?" "Who put the stars there?"

In the ages before writing, these questions were answered on a tribal basis, because adults had them too. The answers were given by the wise ones of the tribe, usually in the form of stories told around the campfire. These stories were passed down from generation to generation. They became the "folk wisdom" of the tribe.

We call these special stories "myths." A myth is not just fiction or "something untrue." Just the opposite. Myths are stories—admittedly fictional—which are designed to embody the deep truths a particular tribe or culture finds fundamental to understanding human life on earth. Obviously, some are better than others. But all should be taken seriously, because all contain a germ of insight common to the human race.

The *Book of Genesis* is composed of myths, but with a difference. When the ancestors of the Jews were telling their stories, God joined them and said, "Let me tell the story." The result was a divinely-inspired myth. A myth designed by God to convey the answers he himself was giving to life's fundamental questions. Each embodies a particular element, not only of Jewish culture, but of God's explanation of the world. We need to look for the meaning each is intended to teach. We do not—emphatically do not—look for precise historical or biological facts. If we read the Bible like a newspaper we will misunderstand everything in it.

What **Genesis 1:1-19** is telling us, essentially, is that God made the world. It isn't just "there"; it is made. It hasn't always existed; it was created at a point in time (more precisely, "time" began when the universe was created). And it was created by a Person. But not an ordinary person like us. Nothing we see has in itself any reason or justification for its own existence. The hand in front of my face has to be explained. There is no reason why it should be there. That already tells us that the origin of creation must be in a Being so different that it doesn't need to be explained—a Being, which, if we could see it, we would realize it could not *not exist*. One that has within itself the cause or source of its own existence because it needs no cause or source; it is Being Itself.

The modern myth of our limited Western culture is the "big bang" theory followed by evolution. Both might be true, but like the technology they came out of, they only explain the process, not the product. Children still ask, "What made the bang go 'bang'?" And how was there anything to go "bang" in the first place? *Genesis* says, "In the beginning, God said...."

Because of *Genesis* we can be at home in the universe. We know it is a gift. To us. From a person. The natural response to this is thanks and praise.[1]

[1] Read Bruce Vawter, *A Path Through Genesis.*

Meditation: Do I take for granted my existence? Should I thank God for it daily?

5

February 8, 2011

Genesis 1:20 to 2:4; Psalm 8; Mark 7:1-13.

O Lord, our God, how wonderful your name in all the earth!

Genesis 1:20 to 2:4 says humans are different from all the rest of creation. God created the earth, sea, and sky; and within their boundaries the plants, fish, and animals, each to act as it was designed to act, according to its nature. And each time God created something, "God saw how good it was."

Everything made sense. Each design "worked." God was happy with the "truth" (intelligibility) and "goodness" (purpose) of every being.

Then God created something better: "Let us make humankind in our image, according to our likeness."

So God created humankind in his image, in the divine image he created them; male and female he created them.

What makes humans different is that we can see what God sees and rejoice in it. We can see why things are put together as they are, understand the mind of their creator, and appreciate them as he does. We realize we are "like God."

Every *being* is identified as *one*—as a unified whole—because each is unified by being structured in a way that is *intelligible* in the light of a *purpose*, or function. Later philosophers would call these the "transcendentals": the traits common to every being that transcend all differences between them. A *being* must be *one, true,* and *good.*

What we say something "is" or *name* it, is *true* only if its various elements ("matter") are in fact intelligible as organized into a working *pattern* ("form") by some competent *agent* to do something the designer perceived as *desirable.* Philosophers call these the "four causes" (explanations) of being: "material, formal, efficient, and final cause." When we "call a spade a spade," we are saying this particular *thing* was *shaped* by *someone* to be *useful* for digging. This is why we call a tree a tree. Or say our body is "human."

There is more. God defined the relationship between humans and the rest of his creatures. Humans are in charge—and responsible; "*Let them have dominion over...* all the living things that move on the earth."

Humans can use the plants and animals:

I have given you every plant yielding seed that is upon the face of all the earth, and every tree... you shall have them for food.... and to everything that has the breath of life, I have given every green plant for food.

But with this comes responsibility for protecting the environment and preserving the order of creation for the well-being of all. In the Mass, *Preface V* for Sundays echoes *Genesis:*

You chose to create humans in your own likeness, setting us over the whole world in all its wonder. You made us the stewards of creation, to praise you day by day for the marvels of your wisdom and power.

An important part of our stewardship is *praise.* Only humans can recognize design and beauty and give thanks. Reading God's word helps us appreciate the privilege of being able to say, *O Lord, our God, how wonderful your name in all the earth.*

Meditation: What does praise add to life? How often do I praise God, others?

6

FEBRUARY 9, 2011

Genesis 2:4-17; Psalm 104; Mark 7:14-23.

Oh, bless the Lord, my soul!

Genesis 2:4-17 tells us God gave humans a responsibility. As "stewards of creation," humans have a job:

> The LORD God planted a garden in Eden... and there he put the man whom he had formed... to cultivate and care for it.

God's word tells us work has the positive value of giving humans dignity. We are not just children playing in a garden. Our lives draw meaning and value from what we do, because what we do has value for the world.

After our fall and redemption, God persists in giving us this dignity. We even have a part in our own salvation:

> You came to our rescue as God, but you wanted us to be saved by one like us. Humans refused your friendship, but a human was to restore it through Jesus Christ our Lord.[1]

Not only that, but Jesus continues to "restore it" through humans who, as his body on earth, continue his mission. There is no end to God's affirmation of human dignity.

Genesis 2:2 said God "rested on the seventh day." This previewed the commandment of the Sabbath rest:

> Remember the sabbath day, and keep it holy. Six days you shall... do all your work. But the seventh day is a sabbath to the LORD; you shall not do any work...For in six days the LORD made heaven and earth but rested the seventh day.[2]

The rabbis explain that this was to teach us we are different. All other creatures exist only for what they contribute to life on the planet. But humans have a reason for existence that precedes and supersedes this: we are created for direct relationship with God. Our *raison d'être* is to know and praise, love and serve God. To keep us conscious of this, God said that one day a week we are not to do anything just because it is useful. Sabbath leisure is an emancipation proclamation. It is freedom from idols.

God laid one restriction on "the man":

> You may freely eat of every tree of the garden; but of the tree of the knowledge of good and evil you shall not eat, for in the day that you eat of it you shall die.

"Knowing good and evil" could mean to make oneself the *criterion*, which is to make oneself like God. The truth is, God intended from the beginning that we should be "like God" in a way beyond imagining. We were created to "become Christ" by Baptism and "in him" to be divine. But not by ourselves. By sharing with others in God's own life, the free gift of "the grace of our Lord Jesus Christ."

This teaches a profound truth about human life. There is no good God does not want to give us. But if we seek any good outside of his guidance and in a way that is against his will, we will diminish rather than enhance our lives. We will "die"—in whole or in part—because the good we seize will not be authentic, will not be whole. It will be flawed and render us flawed. It is only in harmony with God's will that we can say, "*Oh, bless the Lord, my soul!*"

Genesis says we were created to do this.

[1] *Preface III for Sundays.*
[2] *Exodus 20:8-11.*

Meditation: Do I find my value in working, in interacting with God, or in both?

7

FEBRUARY 10, 2011

Genesis 2:18-25; Psalm 128; Mark 7:24-30

Happy are those who fear the Lord.

In **Genesis 2:18-25** the Lord says, "It is not good for the man to be alone. I will make a suitable partner for him." So first he created "various wild animals and birds" and presented them to the man. "Whatever the man called each of them would be its name." This meant the man had the authority to decide what each one would be used for. They were under his control. "But none proved to be the suitable partner for the man."

Authority, controlling others, no matter how benevolently, does not provide the kind of relationship human beings need. Power is not partnership and can never substitute for it.

So God took one of the man's ribs and formed it into a woman. This is not a biology lesson! To take it literally is to miss the meaning of God's story.

When Adam cried out, "This at last is bone of my bones and flesh of my flesh!" it meant he recognized Eve as the "same stuff" that he was; in other words, his equal. Not, as surrounding cultures saw women, something to capture, dominate and use. Adam saw Eve as different: as a partner with whom he could have a human relationship.

Human beings are in the image and likeness of God, not only through endowment with memory, intellect, and will, but because, like the Trinity of Father, Son, and Spirit, their being is not complete without relationship. This is in-scribed in the structure of male and female bodies, neither of which is intelligible except in relation to the other. The Scripture is absolute: "It is not good for humans to be alone."

We are not alone as long as we are in relationship. A hermit monk explained that the difference between loneliness and solitude is relationship: no matter how physically alone we are, we are never lonely as long as we are in deep, loving, recognized relationship with the human race, even if our closest neighbor is a hundred miles away. By contrast, those who relate only through power or control are fundamentally alone even if they are rubbing shoulders with multitudes all day long. They are lonely.

Relationship comes through interaction. But not all interactions create relationships that keep us from being alone. For this we must accept others as "partners," equals with whom we share as equals. What *Genesis* tells us of the relationship between men and women holds for all relationships. To be human, they must be between equals.

Praise is a key to this. It is essential to look for the good in others, affirm it, celebrate it, and rejoice in it. The principle is, "What we do not praise we will not appreciate"—in people or in God. What we do not appreciate we cannot love. So love begins with taking an interest in others: what they know, how they think, the ideals, desires, and choices that make them who they are. And *praising* what is good in them.

Note: we do not really know others until we know their relationship, their interaction, with God.

Meditation: What is good in the people I live with? Work with? Do I affirm it?

FEBRUARY 11, 2011

Genesis 3:1-8; Psalm 31; Mark 7:31-37.

Happy those whose sins are forgiven.

A basic human question is, "Why do people wear clothes?" **Genesis 3:1-8** says it started with sin.

The serpent aroused Eve's interest in the forbidden fruit by promising her it would make humans "like God, knowing good and evil." Her first mistake was to listen. Her second was to take a closer look. What she saw was "good for food, pleasing to the eyes, and desirable for gaining wisdom."

John presents this triple enticement as the basic human temptation: "the desire of the flesh, the desire of the eyes, and the pride of life."[1]

The *Genesis* "good for food," as "desire of the flesh" includes physical gratification, "sensual lust," "disordered bodily desires." We all feel this.

"Pleasing to the eyes," includes the "glamour of evil" we are called to repulse at Baptism when we "reject Satan... and all his empty promises": greed, avarice, uncritical yearning for the visible, short-term goods offered and advertised in every human culture. But we all are partially seduced.

"Enticing for the knowledge or wisdom it could give," goes deeper. "Pride of life" is an arrogant conviction of self-sufficiency, a "complacency and willful independence in pursuing one's earthly existence, pride in one's own resources." This is the opposite of true wisdom, which is defined as the "desire for spiritual things." Our true fulfillment is eternal life, not temporal. Life in union with God. Something we can achieve only in humble obedience and dependence on God. But we often forget this.

Eve fell into the pride of making her own judgment the criterion of truth, and her own choices the source of ultimate fulfillment. This is the core of sin. Adam followed her. And so do we when we skip the guidance of God's word or choose our own will over his.

As a result, our sins let us "know good and evil." That is why, in the Scriptural sense, we "clothe ourselves." We are ashamed of what we are. Afraid to reveal our true selves. Hence the "clothes" of reserve, unsharing privacy, reluctance to express our feelings or thoughts. We are "hung up" out of fear of nakedness.

The answer is not naïve, unrestrained spontaneity. Once sin exists in the world, self-exposure is vulnerability. Jesus did not restore the primitive nakedness of Eden, but he modeled a new nakedness, because nakedness is essential to love. In his ministry Jesus exposed his heart in word and action and his self to rejection. He was naked on the cross as he had made himself naked in self-revelation. But he *loved through it*, shedding his blood "so that sins may be forgiven." When we are naked through love, knowing the risk, love wins.

[1]Translations differ. See *1 John* 2:16 and the 1968 *Jerome Biblical Commentary* for this text and the *Genesis* story.

Meditation: Why am I afraid? Vulnerability is openness to love.

FEBRUARY 12, 2011

Genesis 3:9-24; Psalm 90; Mark 8:1-10.

In every age, you have been our refuge.

For some, the *Responsorial* verse might contradict experience. People blame God precisely because he did not make himself their "refuge" when they needed him. Nations starve. An economic crisis or hurricane strips a family of all they own. A child dies. Do the parents proclaim, *"In every age, O Lord, you have been our refuge"*?

Genesis 3:9-24 provides an answer to this, but often people hear it too late, when emotions make it impossible for them to accept it. Who would blame a parent for being angry with God when a child dies? Certainly God doesn't. It is a natural emotional response. Emotions aren't choices; they just happen.

If, however, one makes an intellectual judgment that God is unloving, this is a free choice. And a self-destructive one. It is also irrational. But people may not be ready to listen to reason when they are in acute distress. That is why it is important to read the word of God: to learn God's explanations of life before we need to know them, so that when we do need them we won't reject them.

The *Genesis* story is a "myth" in which God is telling a deep truth, but with as much independence of scientific or historical truth as a fairy tale. To criticize its biology is as unenlightened as editing the Santa Claus story because reindeer can't fly. We have to look for the point of the story.

God is saying that if there were no sin this world would be a paradise. That is what he made and intended it to be. That is the point; not that God got angry and punished the human race with barren earth and pain in childbearing because our first parents sinned. The story is not about God's emotions. It is about the kind of world God wanted this to be as opposed to the kind of world it is. This is not the world God made; it is the world we have disordered by our sins.

Would there be sickness if there were no sin? If that is a scientific question, the Bible gives no answer. But does God want sickness? The Bible says no.

So why do pain and suffering exist?

Scripture's general answer is, "Because the world is not in harmony with God."

Humans, the "stewards of creation," have not done a good job. Without introducing religion, we can all name a dozen destructive, unhealthy things in the environment that are the demonstrated result of human greed. And, allowing for exceptional miracles, God doesn't intervene. Having made people free, he leaves them free to sin. Having made nature's laws, God stands back when "natural disasters" occur.

Scripture just says, without going into details, that if the natural order of things had not been broken by humans declaring themselves independent of God, all things would be under control. And when humans return to God, "No hurt, no harm will be done on all my holy mountain; for the earth will be full of knowledge of the LORD as the waters cover the sea." (Read all of *Isaiah*, chapter eleven). The root problem is sin; the ultimate answer is love.

Meditation: Am I ready to accept loss, pain, and suffering without blaming God?

FOR REFLECTION AND DISCUSSION: WEEK FIVE

The Fifth Week of Ordinary Time: In *Genesis* God tells stories or "myths" to give his own answers to the basic questions of life. This week tells us humans are *created*, as *equals*, for *relationship* with God and others. We are *in charge* of creation, but *subject* to God, to whom we owe *praise*.

Invitation: To see ourselves and the world through God's eyes.

Ask yourself in prayer and others in discussion, for each statement below: Do you see this in the Scripture reading? What response does it invite?

Genesis 1:1-19 tells us the world isn't just "there." It was created by a Person.

Genesis 1:20 to 2:4: Humans "have dominion" over the rest of creation, but persons, are all equally in God's image, created to relate to each other as "partners."

Humans are the "stewards of creation" to foster life, not death. God wants humans, made in his likeness, to see "how good" all his creatures are and preserve them.

Only rational humans can recognize God's design and intention in created beings. This makes praise an important part of our stewardship.

Genesis 2:4-17: Our lives draw meaning and value from the work we do if our work has value for the world.

God commanded leisure on the Sabbath to teach us that humans have a reason for existence above and beyond what we contribute to life on the planet. We are created for direct relationship with God: to know and praise, love and serve God.

God forbade humans to eat of "the tree of the knowledge of good and evil" because this could make them think they had the right to determine for themselves what is true and good. That is to make oneself the *criterion*, which is the essence of pride.

Genesis 2:18-25: God's point in the "Adam's rib" story is that Adam, recognizing Eve as the "same stuff" that he was, saw her as his equal, a partner.

Human beings are in the image of God because, like the Trinity, our being is not complete without relationship—which requires us to accept and share as equals.

Being in relationship makes the difference between loneliness and solitude. Love begins with taking interest in others, affirming and praising the good in them.

Genesis 3:1-8: Sin makes us hide our true selves under "clothes" of reserve. Expressing our feelings or thoughts makes us vulnerable, but is essential to love.

Genesis 3:9-24: There is suffering because the world is not as God intended it to be. Pain and suffering exist because the world is not in harmony with God.

Meditations:

What does praise add to life? How often do I praise God, others?
Do I experience my value in working, in interacting with God, or both?
Do I affirm what is good in the people I live with? Work with?
Why am I afraid? Vulnerability is openness to love.
Am I ready to accept loss, pain, and suffering without blaming God?

FEBRUARY 13, 2011

Hearing and Living the Word of Life

INVENTORY

Do you think the human race needs guidance in how to live? What about yourself? Where do you look for it? Where has it led you?

INPUT

The author of the *Entrance Antiphon* (*Psalm* 30) speaks in the singular, calling God "*my* rock of refuge, a stronghold to save me." He asks God, "Lead and guide *me*." This invites each of us to ask, "Do I see God's word just as guidance for the human race or the Church in general, or have I accepted it, embraced it as my personal guide, to give direction to my own individual life?"

The *Opening Prayer(s)* recall God has promised to "remain forever" with those who "do what is just and right." But we have to consciously "live in your presence." The wisdom of God's "loving plan" for the human race "took flesh in Jesus Christ." What "changed human history" was "his command of perfect love." If we accept to live "perfect love" we will "reflect God's wisdom" to all around us and "bring salvation to the ends of the earth."

WE CAN CHOOSE

Sirach 15:15-20 tells us it is our choice. We can choose to keep God's command of perfect love or not. We can choose life or death—for ourselves and our society. Scripture promises that "whichever we choose, it will be given to us." God's word assures us, "If you choose you can keep the commandments." To say we can't is a cop-out.

We can't do it by our own strength. Jesus' "new commandment" of perfect love is to "love one another as I have loved you."[1] Who is able to do that? Even for the easier commandments, Scripture doesn't guarantee we can keep them all immediately, just by choosing to. That goes against human experience. Even the pros don't expect to make a touchdown on every play—or to score at all if they don't practice.

The choice to keep the commandments is the choice to train for it.

This is the choice to be a *disciple*. The word "disciple" doesn't mean "follower." Becoming a disciple is what makes us *able* to become a follower. A "disciple" is a "student," an "apprentice Christian" (even though we never actually graduate until we die).

An apprentice is a learner (cp. *aprender* in Spanish and *aprendre* in French: "to learn," both from the Latin *apprehendere*, to "grab." An apprentice is someone who is trying to "get it"). Jesus gives us his "command of perfect love," and we just don't "get it."

Not to be discouraged; the first Pope didn't get it either when Jesus first announced it (see *Matthew* 16:21-23). But that is what time is for. If we just keep trying, eventually we will keep all the commandments. But—and this is extremely important—we have to consciously *choose* this from the outset. We have to "set our hearts" on it. If we sincerely choose the end, we will begin using the means that will enable us to achieve it. One of the first and most essential means is to begin to *read the word of God*. Only a fool would expect to succeed in anything without reading the instructions. But that is commonplace with us!

WE CAN CHOOSE

In **Matthew 5:17-37**, and in all of the "Sermon on the Mount," Jesus is rewriting the Ten Commandments to conform to the "law of perfect love." He does it by changing the goal of the Commandments. Instead of teaching good human behavior that will allow communities to live together in peace, his New Law gives guidelines for living on the level of God himself. Jesus' version of the Commandments teaches the attitudes and values of God's own divine heart. And the assurance of Sirach—"If you choose you can keep the commandments"— although it was not meant to apply to these, is still valid, because now we have the power that comes from sharing in God's own divine life by grace.

Scripture often speaks as if "grace" and the Holy Spirit were not given before Jesus came. They were, of course, because God "who desires everyone to be saved and to come to the knowledge of the truth," was already giving people what would actually be won only through the death and resurrection of Jesus. But these were not recognized or understood until the "grace of the Lord Jesus Christ" was proclaimed and the Spirit was made manifest at Pentecost.[2]

The gift of grace (sharing in God's divine life) is implicitly proclaimed in the Sermon on the Mount, because the ideals Jesus teaches there are simply beyond what human nature of itself can accept or live. If the most we can hope for is to enjoy the good life on this earth, with perhaps the continuance of essentially the same thing in some form after death, there is no motive or justification for the level of love Jesus teaches here.

Everyone condemns murder, because it disrupts society. But Jesus says we must, with our wills, at least, renounce even the anger we feel, because God does not nurse grudges. We cannot call a fool a fool, because in the eyes of God no one is just a fool. It is not enough only to refrain from harming others. Nor can we just ignore those who don't like us. We have to seek reconciliation with anyone who holds something against us.

Why? Because God loves and seeks relationship with every person.

Later (vv. 38-42), Jesus forbids us even to defend ourselves or our property against an aggressor. Why? Because "perfect love" values others and a good relationship with others above all created things: one's property, time, and even one's physical life. This goes beyond the commandment, "Love your neighbor as yourself." Jesus' New Commandment is, "Love one another *as I have loved you*." He revealed the essence of "perfect love" on the cross. "No one has greater love than this, to lay down one's life for one's friends."[3]

We don't have space to show how the whole "Sermon on the Mount" translates the "command of perfect love" into concrete, daily actions.[4] But today's reading shows us Jesus transforming the morality of sex and marriage into a morality of love.

Jesus is not talking about sex. He is talking about how we should look at other persons and ourselves, and live love for both. The idea is to respond as a whole person to whole persons. If we limit our appreciation or desire for another to just one part or aspect of what that person is, this is not perfect love. And if we want to gratify only part of what we are—some particular appetite or part of our body—that is not perfect love for ourselves. If it comes to a choice, we need to sacrifice the part for the sake of the whole rather than lose the wholeness and integrity of our being through absorption in one part.

Jesus rejected the "divorce on demand" sanctioned by the Law. Only the husband could demand it, because the wife was considered his property. And for the same reason, if one spouse had sexual relations with an unmarried person, it was adultery for the wife, but not for the husband: she was his property; he was not hers.[5] Jesus went beyond all this by changing the end (and therefore the nature) of marriage from whatever its

human benefits were to the goal of growing into perfect love. This is the "steadfast love and fidelity" that is the love that defines our very God. If the spouses are learning to love, even a crucifying marriage is a success.

THE SPIRIT EMPOWERS

1Corinthians 2:5-10 calls this the wisdom of the "spiritually mature," not a wisdom "of this age." The New Law of Jesus is something "eye has not seen, ear has not heard, nor the human heart conceived." It is the level of life "God has prepared for those who love him," and who want to love others with his own "perfect love."

But we can live it. God has "revealed this wisdom to us through the Spirit," who "scrutinizes all matters, even the depths of God." The *Responsorial* (*Psalm* 119) says it all: "*Happy are they who follow the law of the Lord.*"

[1]*John 13:34; 15:12.*
[2]*1Timothy 2:4. See John 1:14-18, 7:39; 2Corinthians 13:14.*
[3]*John 15:13.*
[4]For this see my book *Make Me a Sabbath of your Heart.*
[5]See Bishop Geoffrey Robinson, *Confronting Power and Sex in the Catholic Church — Reclaiming the Spirit of Jesus,* Liturgical Press, 2008, pp.185-187.

INSIGHT
Do you see all morality now as an effort to live on the level of God?

INITIATIVE:
Read Scripture daily, trying to understand how God thinks. God is telling us.

FEBRUARY 14, 2011

Genesis 4:1-25; Psalm 50; Mark 8:11-13.

Offer to God a sacrifice of praise.

Genesis 4:1-25 tells the story of the first murder on earth. Brother murders brother, which may be Scripture's way of saying every murder is this. When Cain asks, "Am I my brother's keeper?" the obvious answer is not restricted to blood relations. We are called to love and care for all as brothers and sisters. If we kill anyone, for any reason at all, we need to be aware that it is our brother or sister we are killing. Already, at the very beginning of Scripture, we are told something that should give us second thoughts about the death penalty and war. When we celebrate military victories, we are celebrating the fact that, whether we think it was justified or not, we have killed our brothers and sisters. It is significant that those who have actually been in combat, who have seen the reality first hand, are not the ones most inclined to celebrate.

This reading explains the origin of the blood feud. What deterred people from killing in "primitive" times was the certainty that, if they did, the victim's relatives would come after them and their family until one death resulted in "seven." What does the number mean?

In the Bible it means totality, fullness, completeness. At times it is multiplied by itself (7 X 7 or 7 X 70).... This signifies the removal of limit implied in totality. Thus Cain is avenged 7 times, Lamech 7 X 70 (*Genesis* 4:24).... The 6 days of cre-

ation followed by a 7th day of rest are the complete and perfect work....

In the blood feud killing continues until vengeance is "complete." The Gospels apply the number to forgiveness.

Luke says we should forgive seven times. *Matthew* says 70 X 7. These aren't mathematical statements. Both are saying there should be no limit to the number of times one should forgive.[1]

That is the teaching of Jesus. But in *Genesis* things get worse before they get better. Cain kills his brother out of brooding envy. Lamech boasted later: "I have killed a man for wounding me, a young man for striking me."

Cain is avenged sevenfold, Lamech seventy times sevenfold. By Noah's time there was so much violence God said he was ready to destroy the human race. Then ambition and pride in the building of the Tower of Babel caused such hostility that people divided into separate tribes, separated, and soon lost communication with each other.[2]

In spite of all, God looked at his creation and still "saw how good it was." With faith in the basic goodness of human nature, God continues to give life. "Adam again had relations with his wife, and she gave birth to a son whom she called Seth. 'God has granted me another child in place of Abel,' she said, 'because Cain killed him.'"

When we let God tell the story from his point of view, there is always reason to *"Offer to God a sacrifice of praise."*

[1]John McKenzie, S.J., *Dictionary of the Bible.*
[2]*Genesis* 4:24; 6:13; 11:1-9.

15

FEBRUARY 15, 2011

Genesis 6:5 to 7:10; Psalm 94; Mark 8:14-21

Happy the one you teach, O Lord.

Genesis 6:5 to 7:10: The story of the Flood. Other cultures have flood myths, which we would expect, since most peoples probably remembered some massive inundations in their history, and folk tradition would have taken account of these. The most ancient Middle-East mythologies include stories of both a lost paradise and a deluge. What we have in *Genesis* is God giving his version of these stories, not to provide historical details, but to make them bear the message God wants to deliver.

The message of the flood story is triple: 1. The human race can get so corrupt that it would be understandable if God wished he had never made us. 2. We can never conclude from this that human nature is all bad. Individuals can be different, and "find favor with the Lord," as Noah did. 3. God will not destroy what he has made. He will always leave a "remnant" to continue what he has begun.

The Flood is a survival story. The survival is due to two things: God's own loving intervention, and human willingness to follow his directions out of faith in his word. Noah, as a faithful "steward of creation," preserved both his family and everything for which he was responsible because he *believed* God's word and *obeyed*.

We will see tomorrow that it is also a promise story; one of the bases for the fundamental hope that should characterize human existence.

One immediate lesson we draw from the flood story is the need to read God's word. God doesn't normally speak to people as he did to Noah. But he does speak to every one of us, and in a manner more powerful and reliable than direct revelation:

> In times past God spoke to our ancestors in partial and various ways through the prophets. But in these last days he has spoken to us by a Son, whom he appointed heir of all things, through whom he created the universe.

His message comes to all and to each one of us through the Scriptures. It is double, as it was to Noah. First: "Save yourselves from this corrupt generation." Second: Save everyone God made, by bringing them all into the "Ark," the symbol of the Church.

> The ship (bark or barque, *barchetta*) was an ancient Christian symbol. It is the Church tossed on the sea of disbelief, worldliness, and persecution but finally reaching safe harbor with its cargo of human souls. Part of the imagery comes from the ark saving Noah's family during the Flood (*1Peter* 3:20-21). Jesus protecting Peter's boat and the apostles on the stormy Sea of Galilee (*Mark* 4:35-41). It was also a great symbol during times when Christians needed to disguise the cross, since the ship's mast forms a cross in many of its depictions.[1]

The Church believes that in the *Liturgy of the Word*—or any reading of Scripture—the "Father who is in heaven *meets his children* with great love and *speaks with them.*" The only question is, will we listen? To save ourselves and others? *Happy the one you teach, O Lord.*

[1]*Hebrews* 1:2; 11:7; *Acts* 2:40; *1Peter* 3:20-21; *Matthew* 24:37-39; www.jesuswalk.com/christian-symbols/ship.htm.

Meditation: Do I believe God teaches me personally through Scripture?

FEBRUARY 16, 2011

Genesis 8:6-22; Psalm 116; Mark 8:22-26

Let your hearts take comfort, all who hope in the Lord.

We all live in some fear of "natural disasters"—floods, hurricanes, and the like. Since these are natural, they are not disasters in and of themselves, but only disastrous for any people who happen to have installed themselves where they are bound to occur. We know that the natural movements under the earth will eventually cause an earthquake along the San Andreas Fault in California. People who choose to live there are consciously taking the risk. Some say there is more risk driving on a Los Angeles freeway, and they may be right. But accidents there are called "human errors," while a "natural disaster" is not an error at all, neither human nor divine.

The point of today's reading from **Genesis 8:6-22** is that there is a governance of the universe. The natural things we count on are under God's control and will keep happening:

> As long as the earth endures, seedtime and harvest, cold and heat, summer and winter, day and night, shall not cease.

We take all that for granted, but the Scripture tells us God has guaranteed it. There are laws that govern physical and chemical operations. Everything is not so haphazard and random that we can never know what to expect. Nor is God ever going to fly into a rage and just let nature go wild. When nature appears to us to be going wild, it only means we have not yet figured out its laws.

Scripture adds another dimension we might not stay aware of. We take the sun's rising for granted, or explain it by the earth's revolution, and tend to stop there. God's word, and specifically this passage from *Genesis,* alerts us that nature would not have any laws unless God made them. If nature follows laws, it is because there is Someone in control who is consistent in making things operate the way he designed them to.

Humans appear to be the exception, but even when we disobey what God commands and act contrary to our own natures, God is consistent in leaving our free wills free. One reason he is so tolerant of us is that he accepts our inclination to sin as part of the equation he has recognized since the Fall:

> Never again will I doom the earth because of humankind, since the desires of humans' hearts are evil from the start; nor will I ever again strike down all living beings as I have done.

It isn't as if our sins were a surprise to God! So his love should not surprise us.

The point is that God loves us *as we are,* right now, in spite of our sins. He is as consistent in that as he is in making the sun rise every morning and set every evening. "Summer and winter, day and night" will cease before God's love and care for us will. Isaiah (49:15) tells us that God is more consistent than nature.

> Can a woman forget her nursing child, or show no compassion for the child of her womb? Even these may forget, yet I will not forget you.

By reading God's word we keep in touch with the basic truths of life. That is a reason to do it. *"Let your hearts take comfort, all who hope in the Lord"*—and trust in his enlightenment.

Meditation: Am I aware that God's fidelity is the source of stability in nature?

FEBRUARY 17, 2011

Genesis 9:1-13; Psalm 102; Mark 8:27-33.

From heaven the Lord looks down on the earth.

Genesis 9:1-13: God was tempted to destroy the human race—and with just cause! But Scripture tells us it would not have been consistent with God's character as the Creator and Lifegiver. Now God tells us that we, as formed in his image, must value life as much as he does: in particular the life of any other creature formed in his image; that is, of every human being on earth. As "stewards of creation": we have special responsibility to respect life and to work to enhance the life of every human being living in conditions unworthy of God's image.

> From humans... I will demand an accounting for human life. If anyone sheds human blood, by humans shall that person's blood be shed; for in his own image God made humankind.

There seems to be a contradiction here. If human blood is not to be shed, is God ordering that humans "shall" shed the blood of other humans who do? Murderers are still humans, made in the image of God. Is that image to be respected or not?

When the bishops of the United States declared together, in union with the Pope, that the death penalty should be abolished, were they editing God?

In reading Scripture we have to see "the Father who is in heaven meeting his children with great love and speaking with them." The Father meets his children "where they are at," and speaks to them in ways their present culture and state of development enables them to understand. God is not ordering the execution of killers. He is recognizing that it is going to happen. In the literary form we call "myths," we don't expect literal consistency, even in God's stories. We look for the main point. Here it is the absolute sacredness and inviolability of human life.

In the Flood story, it seems God himself did not respect that. But the point of the story is not whether God actually wiped out people in a flood, but that he promises, "Never again!" And we who are in his image must never do it either. Rather, humans are to foster life: "Be fertile, then, and multiply. Abound on the earth and subdue it." It is clear that humans, who are in the image of God the Creator, are expected to love life, foster it, and make the planet life-friendly. We are in charge, and our first concern should be life. God said:

> "See I am making a covenant with you and your descendants.... with every living creature.... never again shall there be a flood to destroy the earth.... I have set my bow in the clouds, and it shall be a sign of the covenant between me and the earth."

And this, the inspired storyteller told the children around the campfire, "is why there are rainbows. They are a reminder of God's promise."

Who is to say they are not? So we know the physics that explains rainbows. Big deal! When we know the scientific explanation of every phenomenon on earth, we still won't know the half of it. *"From heaven the Lord looks down on the earth."* We need to see what God sees. For this we read his word.

Meditation: Do I feel responsible for fostering and enhancing all life on earth?

FEBRUARY 18, 2011

Genesis 11:1-9; Psalm 33; Mark 8:34-9:1.

Happy the people the Lord has chosen to be his own.

A missionary in Africa noticed a new mud hut outside a village. Asking, he was told "That family did not get along with the chief. They moved out." A few months later there were a dozen new huts. Then there were none. He was told, "A lot of people didn't get along with the chief, so they moved away and started a new village." In a country without writing, it would only be a matter of time before they were speaking a different language.

When children asked, "Grandfather, why don't those other people speak the same language we do?" God gave his answer in **Genesis 11:1-9.**

In the beginning, "the whole world spoke the same language." Then humans discovered how to make bricks. This made tall buildings possible. It went to their head. They decided to build a tower "with its top in the sky" and so "make a name for ourselves." Technology is good, but can come from ambition and lead to pride.

We said above that humans' first temptation was to make themselves, not God, the *criterion* of right and wrong. This reading's temptation is similar, and it dominates our technological culture. We think that whatever we discover how to do we have a right to do—from nuclear warfare to biogenetics. If we limit ourselves to physics without going "beyond physics" to "metaphysics," the only "natural laws" we will know are scientific laws. If we also exclude God's laws, technology is a loose cannon.

People without God's law, motivated by pride and ambition, are bound to fight. When they do, they will have to separate. Soon, even if they use the same words, they won't "speak the same language." The result is a fragmented world, destructive to human life.

The story attributes this natural consequence to God, as Scripture often does. But God did not cause the discord. God's own action is always unifying. At Pentecost, when the apostles preached to people gathered from different countries, by the power of the Spirit "each one heard them speaking in the native language of each." This was a preview of the reversal of Babel, when people will all be one, speaking the "language of the Spirit."[1]

Ironically, the builders of Babel thought it would protect them from being "scattered all over the earth." But their effort to protect themselves and their society from dissolution without God had the opposite effect. Our reliance on the technology of military power will have the same result. Christians know it is union with Jesus himself that ultimately brings peace to all. Christ himself said, "Whoever does not gather with me scatters." God's "plan for the fullness of time" is to "gather up all things in Christ, things in heaven and things on earth." He does it, not by force, but by offering himself in love. We must do likewise. *Happy the people the Lord has chosen to be his own.*[2]

[1]See *Acts* 2:1-7; *Isaiah* 2:1-5.
[2]*Matthew* 12:30; *Ephesians* 1:10; 2:13-14.

Meditation: What causes division in your world? What would overcome it?

FEBRUARY 19, 2011

Hebrews 11:1-7; Psalm 145; Mark 9:2-13.

I will praise your name forever, Lord.

The liturgy ends the readings from *Genesis* (until Week 12) with a final reading from **Hebrews 11:1-7**; probably because *Genesis* calls us to see the world through eyes of faith and this reading holds up three exemplary models of faith from *Genesis*: Abel, Enoch, and Noah.

Faith is "conviction about things we do not see." This is what *Genesis* gave us:

> By faith we understand that the worlds were prepared by the word of God, so that what is seen was made from things that are not visible.

Abel "by faith offered to God a more acceptable sacrifice than Cain's, and for that he was acknowledged as upright."

Enoch and Noah both "walked with God" (*Genesis* 5:22-24; 6:9). Because *Genesis* (ch. 5) says "Then he died" about all on the list of Adam's descendants except Enoch, *Hebrews* concludes, "Enoch was taken away without dying." He "walked with God; then was seen no more, because God took him." The fruit of his faith.

Scripture testifies Enoch was "pleasing to God," which is "impossible without faith." Anyone who "comes to God must believe that he exists and that he rewards those who seek him."

Noah "by faith, warned about things not yet seen... built an ark that his household might be saved." His faith in an invisible warning without visible support "was a judgment on the world, and he was able to claim the uprightness which comes through faith."

This passage seems to offer a practical response to all we have seen in *Genesis*. The message is, "Live by faith in the invisible truths you learn from God's word." What we see with our eyes can teach us much, but not enough. In the story of creation, God's words cast light on the visible by revealing what is invisible to us but visible to God.

To benefit from God's words, however—and to "get something" from the *Liturgy of the Word*—we have to do three things: *Read, Reflect,* and *Respond.* And we have to do all of these with *faith.* "For just as the body without the spirit is dead, so faith without works is also dead." But reading God's word fosters faith. John ends his Gospel:

> Jesus did many other signs... not written in this book. But these are written *so that you may come to believe* that Jesus is the Messiah, the Son of God, *and that through believing* you may have life in his name.[1]

If the *Genesis* story did nothing else, it should move us to praise. People who do not know the world was created have lost the capacity to praise anyone for it. You can't praise blind chance (if you are philosophically naïve enough to believe in it). Undirected evolution can be intriguing but not praiseworthy. If everything began with an unexplained "big bang" posited by default, there is nothing we can truly "admire" in nature, and no one to praise, either for the product or the process. *Genesis* empowers us to say with both reason and faith: *I will praise your name forever, Lord.*

[1]*James* 2:26; *John* 20:30-31.

Meditation: What does faith add to the visible world that moves you to praise?

FOR REFLECTION AND DISCUSSION: WEEK SIX

The Sixth Week of Ordinary Time tells us God the Creator wills life, not death. And so should we, being made in God's image and consecrated "stewards of creation."

Invitation: To enhance life on earth in every way we can.

Ask yourself in prayer and others in discussion, for each statement below: Do you see this in the Scripture reading? What response does it invite?

Genesis 4:1-25: If we kill anyone, we need to be aware that it is our brother or sister we are killing. We are called to love and care for all as brothers and sisters.

God continues to give life because he looks at his creation and still sees "how good it is." We need to have faith in the basic goodness of human nature.

Genesis 6:5 to 7:10: The Flood story tells us that no matter how corrupt the human race becomes God will not destroy us or anything he has made. We can never conclude from sins that human nature is just bad. Individuals can be different.

In the Flood story, survival is due to two things: God's own loving intervention, and human willingness to follow his directions out of faith in his word.

Genesis 8:6-22: Nature has and follows laws because there is Someone in control. "Natural disasters" are not disasters in themselves, but only for people who happen to have installed themselves where they are bound to occur.

Genesis 9:1-13: The point is not whether God actually wiped out people in a flood, but that God says destroying humanity is something he will never do. Killing is inconsistent with God's character as Creator.

We who are in the image of God the Creator, are expected to make the planet life-friendly. We are in charge, and our first concern should be life.

Genesis 11:1-9: In our technological culture we think that whatever we *can* do we have a right to do—from nuclear warfare to biogenetics. People motivated by pride and ambition are bound to fight. When they do, they have to separate. The result is a fragmented world, destructive to human life.

Hebrews 11:1-7: Three exemplary figures from *Genesis* encourage us to live by faith in the invisible truths we learn from God's word. To benefit from God's words, we have to *Read, Reflect,* and *Respond.* And do all of these with *faith.*

If the *Genesis* story did nothing else, it should move us to praise. People who do not know the world was created have lost the capacity to praise anyone for it.

Meditations:

What does God's view teach me about life and death?
Do I believe God teaches me personally through Scripture?
Am I aware that God's fidelity is the source of stability in nature?
Do I feel responsible for fostering and enhancing all life on earth?
What causes division in your world? What would overcome it?
What does faith add to the visible world that moves you to praise?

FEBRUARY 20, 2011
Accepting the New Commandment

INVENTORY

Today, is it possible to be fully human without being "fully divine"? What, for a Christian, does it mean to "be holy"? What does it mean to "be perfect"? Can we?

INPUT

The *Entrance Antiphon* (*Psalm* 13) focuses us on God's love and faithfulness: "I will sing to the Lord for his goodness to me." This is the focus we ask for in the *Opening Prayer*: "Father, keep before us the wisdom and love you have revealed in your Son." They are the same: the height of God's wisdom and love were both revealed in the "foolishness" of the cross and Christ's insistence that to be his disciples we must "endure evil with love" as he did.[1] The alternate *Opening Prayer* leads us to discipleship: "Faith in your word is the way to wisdom, and to ponder your divine plan is to grow in truth." This is what the *Liturgy of the Word* invites.

[1] *1 Corinthians* 1:18-25; *Matthew* 16:21-25.

BE HOLY AS GOD

Leviticus 19:1-18: We sometimes speak as if the God of the Jewish Scriptures (Old Testament) and of the Christian Scriptures (New Testament) were two different Gods: the first a God of vengeance and violence; the second a God of mercy and gentleness. But they are one and the same God. It is just that when God reveals himself to humans, the pure light of his Truth and Being comes to us shining through the filter of human cultural assumptions and prejudices.

It is God's pure light; and even when it "shines in the darkness," the darkness "cannot overcome it."[1] But we have to understand that, when God speaks through human beings, he speaks *as* those human beings speak. God doesn't bypass their humanity and shine through them as through perfectly transparent glass that has no color of its own. If God wanted to do that, he would not use human instruments at all, but just make his own words appear on paper somewhere, or write them on a wall. Then they would be exactly the same for all time, and there would be no cultural influence on them except for the language they were written in. Some "people of the Book" (Jews, Christians, and Muslims, who all believe in one God revealing himself in the words of the Bible) want to exclude the cultural influence by insisting on a "sacred language" which alone can authentically transmit God's thought as no "vernacular" translation can. Whether we think God only speaks Hebrew, Arabic, or Latin, we are misunderstanding the nature of revelation. God reveals himself equally in all languages and in none. He identifies with the person he is inspiring to write, and expresses himself in and through that person in a way consistent with that individual's own culture and personality. Matthew's mother, hearing his Gospel, would have recognized immediately, "That's my boy!"

God makes sure, however, that there will be no distortion of what he is actually saying, even though we may have difficulty at times distinguishing the content from the form of its expression. This is particularly true when the "literary form" is storytelling or interpretation of historical events.

Sometimes, however, God speaks about himself and about who and what he is, in a way that seems to escape all the cultural filters like rays of the sun shining through a break in the clouds. Today's reading is like that.

"Be holy, for I the LORD your God am holy." This is pure God! Different cultures might understand differently what "holy" means, but the principle stands in all of them.

When *Leviticus* gets concrete and goes into detail about it, we see both cultural elements and elements that transcend cultural limitations. The first of the omitted verses says, speaking absolutely, "Do not turn to idols." That follows from the Great Commandment of all monotheistic religions that recognize God as God: "Hear, O Israel: The LORD is our God, the LORD alone. You shall love the LORD your God with all your heart, and with all your soul, and with all your might."[2] But the second half of the sentence, "or make cast images for yourselves," was only a particular means to the first which, while necessary in a culture surrounded by people who worshiped statues, is no longer relevant in a culture like ours, where idolatry takes a different form. We make statues of heroes, beauties, and saints, but we don't worship any of them. Unfortunately, we don't make statues of the values we do worship—power, technology, affluence, sex, sports, etc.— and so we do not recognize them as idols.

When God is quoted as assigning punishments for violations of particular commandments, these are not intended as revelations of the nature of God. They don't say God is a punisher. They say, in language, images, and actions that would help the people of the time understand, "This is really bad. If you do this, bad stuff is going to happen." We do the same thing when we try to warn children away from dangerous actions by making up all sorts of fictitious consequences to scare them with because they can't understand or appreciate the real consequences.

When *Leviticus* gets to the verses quoted in the reading, however, this is too far above every human ideal to be an expression of culture. God is telling us how to be "holy as God is holy":

> You shall not bear hatred for your brother or sister in your heart.... Take no revenge and cherish no grudge.... You shall love your neighbor as yourself.

The reason given is, "I am the LORD." This is how God is, so this is how we need to be. The *Responsorial* (*Psalm* 103) says, "*The Lord is kind and merciful*"; that is, "Be kind and merciful for I the Lord your God am kind and merciful." No cultural filter here.

BE PERFECT IN LOVE

In the Sermon on the Mount Jesus takes the Old Law to a new level, transforming it from rules of good human behavior to guidelines for living on the level of God. But what he says in **Matthew 5:38-48** is already basically present in the reading from *Leviticus*. He simply makes more clear and explicit what it means to "be holy as I the Lord your God am holy." It means, above all, to live out his command of "perfect love." By the gift of sharing in God's divine life (the definition of "grace"), we are called and enabled to "be perfect as our heavenly Father is perfect." Since "God is love," to be perfect like God is to be perfect in love.[3]

Genesis says God "looked at everything he had made, and he found it very good." This is even more true of humans, created in the image of God himself. So Jesus is teaching us to love like God when he tells us we need to love one another and value relationship with one another more than all created things:

> • more than our *possessions* ("give to everyone who begs or wants to borrow from you;" if someone wants to steal the shirt off your back, "hand over your coat as well");
> • more than our *time* (if someone imposes, go the "extra mile");
> • more than our desire to avoid *hurt* and rejection ("turn the other cheek").

Jesus says "offer no resistance to one who is evil" for the sake of holding on to any created thing. "My command to you is: love your enemies, pray for your persecutors."

YOU ARE THAT TEMPLE

This command is beyond human goodness. But in **1Corinthians 3:16-23** Paul catches us up short in our objections: "Do you not know that you are God's temple and that God's Spirit dwells in you?... God's temple is holy, and you are that temple." Because we are holy, we have to act like God. This means loving one another, not just as ourselves, but according to the "new commandment" Jesus gave: "Love one another *as I have loved you.*"[4]

By human cultural standards, the love Jesus orders is crazy. But we are not just human; we are divine. Our whole standard of judgment is different. Paul writes: "The wisdom of this world is foolishness with God." And vice-versa: the "wisdom and love" revealed in the crucified Jesus is foolishness to this world. No one who has the power to kill an enemy will choose to be killed instead. But we call that "perfect love."

[1] *John* 1:5.
[2] *Deuteronomy* 6:4-5.
[3] *1John* 4:8,16.
[4] *John* 13:34; 15:12; *Romans* 13:8; *1John* 4:7-12.

INSIGHT
Do you trust more in your "gut" cultural instincts or in God's word?

INITIATIVE:
Seek "wisdom and love" through reflection on God's word. Set a time.

February 21, 2011

Begin Sirach; Psalm 93; Mark 9:14-29.

The Lord is king; robed in majesty.

In *Genesis* God's story about creation gave us "a version with vision." Now the *Liturgy of the Word* invites us to go beyond basic understanding and explore the deep *wisdom* literature that teaches us to live in this world with "appreciation for spiritual things."

Sirach is also known as *Ecclesiasticus* ("church book") because of the use the early Christians made of it for moral teaching. It was written by Jesus Ben Sira around 180 B.C. The Christians accepted it in the "canon" or list of inspired books, but after the first century the Jews did not. Protestant Bibles include it in the "Apocrypha" or "Deuterocanonical Books." Ben Sira presents it as "wise instruction, appropriate proverbs," to feed *discipleship*: "*Wise the one who meditates upon these things, who takes them to heart. One who puts them into practice can cope with anything, having the fear of the Lord for a lamp*" (51:27).

Sirach 1:1-10 begins by saying, "*All wisdom comes from the Lord.*" Who would dispute that? But if we *really* believed it, we would be seeking wisdom where it can be found: in God's word and in the reflections on God's word that the saints, "doctors of the Church," and spiritual writers have handed down to us over the centuries. And in deep reflection and discussions, guided by faith, about our daily experience. But how much time do how many people spend doing this? Who "*meditates upon these things*"?

Let's be honest: Do you yourself really value the wisdom that "comes from the Lord"? You certainly value the cultural education that comes from and prepares for life in this world. You spent hours of every day in school for years to acquire it. What in your life shows as clearly that you value divine wisdom?

How much of the knowledge you spent your time acquiring has any long-term value? For the life that begins with death, the life we were created for, all of our cultural, technological knowledge will be as useful as a high school letter jacket to a college student. Or a play toy to an adult. Something that belonged to another life; that has no relevance now.

Forget death. Without the wisdom that comes from God, we can't deeply appreciate life in the world around us. We have fantastic technology. It makes us more comfortable, healthy, and effective both in preserving and destroying life. But all it tells us is how things work; nothing about what we can become as human persons through the use of them. Wisdom teaches that.

Ben Sira says wisdom is ours for the seeking. The Lord "*has lavished her upon his friends.*" We know that "in Christ Jesus" the eternal Word of God "became for us wisdom from God." Wisdom incarnate.[1] Jesus' words and actions display wisdom before our eyes. How much time do we spend on them? We all recite dutifully at Mass, "*The Lord is king; he is robed in majesty.*" Is he for me?

[1] *1Corinthians* 1:30.

Meditation: Ask deeply and honestly, "Who is God for me?"

FEBRUARY 22, 2011

The Chair of St. Peter, Apostle

The *Responsorial (Psalm 23) "The Lord is my shepherd; there is nothing I shall want"* lifts up our eyes to heaven. This feast brings them down to earth. We are celebrating the "Chair" or official function of St. Peter in the Church and of those elected to represent him in continuing it: the bishops of Rome. This confronts us with the central mystery of Christianity: the Word made flesh, God made human in Jesus Christ.

This is also the central mystery of the Church: a human organization that is also the divine body of Christ. A community of sinful human beings, governed by sinful human beings, that nevertheless proclaims itself—and is— "holy" and guided by the Holy Spirit.

For all the centuries of the Church's life, both in abstract theology and in practical spirituality, the pendulum has swung back and forth between the divine and the human, emphasizing one at the expense of the other, both in Christ and in the Church. The Church's answer, both in doctrine and in constantly reformed practice, has been to keep reaffirming the ancient formula: Jesus is "fully human and fully divine." And in the measure that it is possible, so is and must be his Church.

Nothing calls this more into question than the papacy: the "Chair of Peter." Pope Paul VI said, "The Pope... is undoubtedly the gravest obstacle in the path of ecumenism."[1]

Peter, the first pope, has more recorded sins and errors than any other person in the Gospels. He comes across in the Gospels as a leader, yes, but with a right-to-wrong ratio of two to seven, with one

split decision. He was right when he confessed Jesus to be the Messiah (twice). He was wrong when:

• he rejected Jesus' way of saving the world;
• he misunderstood the transfiguration;
• he presumed Jesus would pay a temple tax;
• he objected to Jesus' washing his feet;
• he protested he would never deny Jesus;
• he slept during Jesus' agony in the garden;
• he opted for violence when Jesus was arrested.[2]

Peter showed cowardice, both in his denial of Jesus in the garden, and later, even after the strengthening of Pentecost, in his government of the Church. Paul reports he "opposed him to his face" for his hypocrisy.[3]

In **Matthew 16:13-19** Jesus praised Peter for his confession of faith: "Blessed are you, Simon son of Jonah! For flesh and blood has not revealed this to you, but my Father in heaven." And he gave him "the keys of the kingdom of heaven." Peter's first act after that was to reject Jesus' teaching on an issue so vital that Jesus called him the devil! "Get behind me, Satan! You are a stumbling block to me; for you are setting your mind not on divine things but on human things." In this passage Peter spoke first as divine, then as human, almost in the same breath.

We don't like to deal with the tension between the human and the divine in the Church. Most Catholics prefer to assume that all popes are holy men (we call them all "Your Holiness") and that we can trust their judgment both in matters of doctrine and of Church government. But this in itself is a denial of the faith! My class learned in the fifth grade that the pope is only infallible when he explicitly defines a doctrine "*ex cathedra*," speaking from the "Chair of Peter" with all his authority, which he has done only twice in history. Many Catholics today keep proving they are "not smarter than a fifth grader."

We simply must accept the human as well as the divine in the Church and in the papacy. Archbishop John Quinn introduced his book *The Reform of the Papacy* by referring to John Paul II's encyclical on Christian unity, *Ut Unum Sint*: "For the first time it is the Pope himself who raises and legitimizes the question of reform and change in the papal office in the Church. [He] calls for a widespread discussion of how this reform could be brought about...."[4]

A key forerunner in this process was Father J.M.R. Tillard, O.P., whose book *The Bishop of Rome* resulted from multiple ecumenical dialogues between Catholic, Protestant, and Orthodox Commissions seeking mutual understanding. There is a new desire for and movement toward unity. The problem is not the primacy of the "Chair of Peter," but the way it is understood and exercised at present in Rome. "The present Catholic vision of the papacy magnifies the office. It makes the pope more than a pope." A joint Lutheran-Catholic declaration accepts the tension between human and divine.

The centralization of the Petrine function in a single person or office results from a long process of development.... The papal office can be seen both as a response to the guidance of the Spirit in the Christian community, and also as an institution which, in its human dimensions, is tarnished by frailty and even unfaithfulness.

One obvious source of this, given perennial human sinfulness, is the corrupting force of *power*, whether possessed or desired. Bishop Geoffrey Robinson addresses this in his reflections on nine years of official leadership in dealing with child-abuse:

Those years left an indelible mark on me.... A number of people, at every level, were seeking to 'manage' the problem and make it 'go away', rather than truly confront and eradicate it. Through all this I came to the unshakeable conviction that within the Catholic Church there absolutely must be profound and enduring change. In particular... on the two subjects of *power* and *sex*.

Do we want to hear this? Do we want to accept and deal with the ever-present human factor in the divine body of Christ on earth? Or do we prefer to just ignore it and hope it will "go away"? The Second Vatican Council answers:

This Synod urges all concerned to work hard to prevent or correct any abuses, excesses or defects which may have crept in here or there, and to restore all things to a more ample praise of Christ and of God.[5]

Catholics are so certain of God's divine preservation and guidance of the Church that, as G.K. Chesterton said of Thomas Aquinas, we dare to walk on the very precipice of issues challenging our faith, confident that truth, if confronted, will always justify belief. Like St. Paul, like Pope John Paul II, Bishops Quinn and Robinson, Fr. Tillard and other theologians, we show our faith in the "Chair of Peter" by constantly calling those who sit on it to fidelity.

In 1Peter 5:1-4 it is Peter himself who invites us to see him, not as a monarch on his throne, nor as someone separated from us by exalted status in the Church, but as a "fellow elder," identified above all as "a witness of Christ's sufferings" and, like all who believe, a "sharer in the glory that is to be revealed."

The glory he speaks of is divine. It is not to be projected in the Church in any human form here on earth. This warning is addressed specifically to the "elders," "presbyters," the preferred designation in Scripture and current Church theology for those in Holy Orders whom we are accustomed to call "priests."[6]

Peter says the clergy are to be "examples to the flock, not lording it over those assigned to you." Obviously, the corrupting influence of power was already visible in the infant Church. If Lord Acton's axiom is true: "Power corrupts and absolute power corrupts absolutely," we should above all guard the clergy against this. Bishop Robinson warns: "To give great authority to a person who is incapable of handling it in a responsible manner is to invite problems.... Spiritual power is arguably the most dangerous of all.... If the governing image of how to act as a priest... is tied to the idea of lordship and control, then, no matter how benevolently ministry is carried out, an unhealthy domination and subservience will be present."[7]

Jesus warned his Church not to be like the "scribes and Pharisees who sit on the Chair of Moses." They "lord it over the flock" through *dress*, *titles*, and *protocol*.

They make their phylacteries broad and their fringes long... love to have the place of honor at banquets and the best seats in the synagogues, and to be greeted with respect in the marketplaces, and to have people call them rabbi.

Father Bernard Häring, C.SS.R., whose eye-opening work *The Law of Christ* makes him arguably the founder of modern Gospel-based moral theology, wrote that at the "very last session" of the Second Vatican Council:

several cardinals, patriarchs, bishops, and some theologians, including myself, were gathered to discuss a final proposal.... that the Council Fathers should not return to their respective dioceses without first having solemnly pledged apostolic poverty and, above all, apostolic simplicity by renouncing all anti-evangelical titles.... Several hundred bishops were ready for this step. However, time was pressing and the proposal never came to pass.[8]

When the hierarchy first began to assume the trappings of secular power—pretentious titles, imposing dress, and a protocol that isolated them above the "common herd"—would Jesus have said to them, "Blessed are you, for flesh and blood has not revealed this to you, but my Father in heaven," or "You are an obstacle to me; you are thinking, not as God does, but as human beings do"?

Celebrating the Chair of Peter invites us to reflect on the alerts from these prophetic, ordained bishops and holy, approved theologians who are part of the *magisterium* of the Church.

[1]Speech to the Secretariat for Christian Unity, April 28, 1967.
[2]See *Matthew* 14:20-31; 16:16, 22; 17:4, 25; 26:35, 40; *John* 6:8; 26:22; 18:40. The split decision was walking on the water with faith, and then almost drowning for lack of faith.
[3]*Galatians* 2:11-14.
[4]Crossroad, 1999, pp. 13-14.
[5]Tillard: Michael Glazier, Inc., 1986, pp. 8-9, 19. Robinson: *Confronting Power and Sex in the Catholic Church*, Liturgical Press, 2008, "Introduction." Vatican II: *The Church*, no. 51.
[6]See Bishop Patrick Dunne of Auckland, *Priesthood: A Re-examination of the Roman Catholic Theology of the Presbyterate*, Alba House, 1990, p. 110.
[7]*op. cit.*, p. 12.
[8]*Priesthood Imperiled*, Triumph/Ligouri, 1996, p. 48.

Meditation: What am I doing to swell or shrink the sense of power in the Church?

(SAME DAY)

Sirach 2:1-11; Psalm 37; Mark 9:30-37.

Commit your life to the Lord.

A once-popular love song begins, "I never promised you a rose garden." **Sirach 2:1-11**, however, does. But he is honest about the thorns. To those who *"come to serve the Lord"* he says, *"Prepare yourself for trials."* Good and evil are at war in our world, and in each one's heart. If you get into the fight, you are going to get hit. Be ready for it.

For in fire gold is tested, and those who are worthy in the crucible of humiliation.

If we *"cling to the Lord,"* however, and *"forsake him not,"* he promises, *"Your future will be great."* If we persevere. God wins. *Sirach* says, "Look around!"

Study the generations long past and understand. Has anyone hoped in the Lord and been disappointed?

A key to the consolation of the spiritual life is *commitment.* Just knowing we are *"sincere of heart and steadfast"* in our determination to grow as disciples is a mystical experience. Where could this determination come from if not grace? And if from grace, we are responding to a personal call from God. We are experiencing God; we are in live, interactive contact with him. God is speaking and we are responding. That is a mystical experience.

Commitment, however, is only realized *"in the crucible of humiliation."* We don't realize we are determined to be faithful until we don't feel like it any more. It is humiliating not to feel "holy" anymore, because on the emotional level we no longer want to do what we promised, but it takes this to experience commitment as pure gold.

When this happens we gain a double clarity: we are able to see the difference, first, between our emotions and our choices. Second, between what comes from us and what comes from God.

When our emotions don't support our will, we realize we are fragmented beings. We say with St. Paul, "I see in my members another law at war with... my mind, making me captive to the law of sin.... Wretched human that I am!" But if we are at war, something in us must be fighting for the good. My "bad self" reveals my "good self"!

Paul cries, "Who will rescue me from this body of death?" And he answers, "Christ our Lord!" By persevering we realize our strength and virtue are not from us alone, but from "the grace of the Lord Jesus Christ" living within us.[1]

So the first step into discipleship is *"Commit your life to the Lord."* Declare yourself a learner, an apprentice follower of Jesus. That makes our Christianity a conscious choice to "come to serve the Lord." Have you had that experience?

A live root branches out. So the decision to enroll as a student in the school of Christ must take visible form in concrete commitments. How will I start? Will I read Scripture? Join a discussion group? Use the sacrament of Reconciliation as a "progress report" for sustaining growth? Read other books? Get to daily Mass? Make the Cursillo? Go on retreat? Take a course? *What? When?* and *How?* make choices real.

[1]*Romans 7:23 to 8:2.*

Meditation: Do I really choose to *"Commit my life to the Lord"*? Why?

FEBRUARY 23, 2011

Sirach 4:11-19; Psalm 119; Mark 9:38-40.

O Lord, great peace have they who love your law.

What advantage is there in embracing discipleship? What does "wisdom" give us? **Sirach 4:11-19** lists some advantages:

Wisdom *"instructs her children and admonishes those who seek her."* Disciples want, and get, input: both general instruction and insight into their own failings. Those who want wisdom *"love life,"* because they want to grow into more life, into *"life to the full."*[1]

Those who seek wisdom *"win her [God's] favor"* just by *desiring* to grow. But to be authentic, desire has to pass into action. And only those who "hold her fast" through perseverance will "inherit glory." Perseverance is the measure of desire. Still, wherever we are along the way, *"the Lord bestows blessings."* God rewards us from the moment we take the first step.

Discipleship enhances our life, but it is not just self-serving. *"Those who serve her [wisdom] serve the Holy One."* We were created "to know, love, and serve God." To try to grow in knowledge and love is to serve God.

Discipleship is not just one-sided self-improvement. God is involved. *"Those who love her [wisdom], the Lord loves."* Reading Scripture is live interaction with God who "In the sacred books...*meets his children* with great love and *speaks with them."* God has a special love for those who love truth and goodness enough to seek to grow in them. He "fills them with life and goodness" and "makes them holy."[2]

Those who *"hearken"* to what God tells them will *"dwell in the inmost chambers"* of God's heart. Jesus said, "Those who love me will keep my word, and my Father will love them, and *we will come to them and make our home with them."* The fruit of discipleship is *union.* Ultimately, it is the perfect union of the "spiritual marriage" which is the goal of a prayerful Christian life.[3]

We need to decide what we trust in to lead us to the fullness of life—here as well as hereafter. *Sirach* says that those who *"trust her [wisdom]"* to do this *"will possess her."* St. Thomas Aquinas defines wisdom as "appreciation for spiritual things." It takes wisdom to seek wisdom. We experience it when we consciously, deliberately, deeply decide and *choose* to become *disciples,* "students," of Jesus Christ, Wisdom Incarnate; Teacher of Truth and Goodness; the Way, the Truth, and the Life. If we choose this, not only will we possess wisdom; our "descendents too will inherit her." There is no greater heritage to pass on to our children.[4]

When we are "strangers," the path of wisdom may lead us *through* "fear," but it leads *to* "happiness." Wisdom *"tries"* us until our hearts are *"fully with her,"* because God only gives All for all.

[1]*John* 10:10.
[2]Vatican II, "Liturgy," no. 33. See the ending of *Eucharistic Prayer I*, speaking of God's gifts.
[3]See Teresa, *Interior Castle*, Dwellings V to VII; *Ephesians* 5:25-32.
[4]*John* 14:6.

Meditation: Do I truly want "wisdom"? Enough to become a disciple?

FEBRUARY 24, 2011

Sirach 5:1-10; Psalm 1; Mark 9:41-50.

Happy are they who hope in the Lord.

Discipleship is about *conversion*. Why should God give us light if we don't intend to walk by it? Jesus is identified as Light and Life interchangeably: "In him was life, and the life was the light of all people...."[1]

When we meditate on Scripture, what opens the door to its meaning is a *practical focus*. The three "R's" of Scriptural meditation are "Read, Reflect, Respond." Sometimes our reflection seems barren: we don't get any great thoughts. No problem. Just ask, "What can I *do* to express belief in what I have just read?" Look for a concrete action, no matter how trivial it seems. And do it. Then you will have meditated successfully on Scripture.

And you will probably have found the key to the real meaning of the passage.

Oddly, meditation requires us to make decisions with confidence, but depends on recognized powerlessness. When God calls us to something, if we think we can do it, we haven't understood the full dimensions of the "it." God calls us to do what God alone can do, and we only by union with him in grace. We need to look for the divine dimension even in ordinary decisions.

Sirach 5:1-10 says, *"Rely not on your wealth; say not, 'I have the power.'"* Here "wealth" means anything that enables human action on earth: wealth of knowledge, talent, energy, resources: none enables us to live or act on the level of God.

Only responsive union and interaction with God sharing his own divine life with us does that. Jesus is the vine, we the branches. Apart from him we can do nothing.[2]

"Rely not on your strength in following the desires of your heart." Will power is not enough. To think so is the fast track to discouragement. If we don't invest time in prayer, the rest of our time will be wasted. Most of us learn this the hard way. Prayer is not our first priority.

"Delay not your conversion to the Lord. Put it not off from day to day." We intend to "get more religious" *someday*. When the pressure eases up or we have more time, have become accepted in a group, made a team, made some money. Sirach answers: "Some day, dumb day!" So does Jesus.[3] Before that day comes, you will have wasted half your life.

When Ben Sira says, *"Of forgiveness be not overconfident,"* he is not putting limits on God's mercy. He is just telling us how it works. God "has mercy" by empowering us to *act*. If we don't, we reap the fruit of whatever we do or don't do. God forgives us whenever we turn to him. He "takes away" all our sins, as if we had never committed them. But lost time is lost time. Jesus promised we would "bear fruit, fruit that will last." But not if we don't plant. Not if we don't receive his word in prayer, water and weed around it.[4]

"Happy are they who hope in the Lord." They "yield their fruit in its season." The season is now.

[1] *John* 1.4, 12.
[2] *John* 15:5.
[3] *Luke* 12:15-59; *Matthew* 5:25.
[4] *John* 15:16; *Matthew* 13:3-23; *Galatians* 6:6-10.

Meditation: What am I waiting for? What do I intend to do "someday"?

FEBRUARY 25, 2011

Sirach 6:5-17; Psalm 119; Mark 10:1-12.

Guide me, Lord, in the way of your commands.

When we see the paths people follow in this world, what overwhelms us is the seductive power of culture.

Children grow up in Christian homes. Their parents have the faith and form them in it. But once out of the house, they stop going to Mass. The last thing on earth youth want to hear is that they are "conformists." But in fact, their behavior is predictable. They conform to the attitudes, and values of their peer group. First in college; later in business and politics.

They were taught Jesus is the Way, the Truth, and the Life. But they follow the way of the world, accept the truth filtered through their society, and their life is like everyone else's.

They think they are free and different, but they are only free from the truth the Church teaches and different from their parents. They accept uncritically the rules of their chosen environments and blend into the scenery. They don't stand out.

Sirach 6.5-17 is realism. If we think we are free spirits we are naïve. It is true we form ourselves as persons by our choices. But it is also true that our choices are all influenced, and most of them pre-determined, by the communal choices of our peer group. So *Sirach* says, *"Choose your friends."* When we do, we are in fact choosing our way of life, whether or not we are aware of it. Do you find this hard to believe?

Language: what words do you find acceptable and why? *Dress*: who chose the image you are projecting? *Food and drink*: how original are your habits? *Spending*: what are your thought-out priorities? *Family life*: How is yours visibly different from others; what sets the daily schedule? *Housing*: what is the "right" kind of neighborhood? *Work*: what determined your choice of career? *Work-ethic*: whose rhythm are you dancing to? *Reading*: who are your favorite authors? *Conversation*: what do you talk about? Avoid talking about? *Morality*: What is acceptable: in your work, social life, political choices? Does your behavior raise eyebrows among your peers? Make them uncomfortable?

"When you gain friends, first test them. And be not too ready to trust them." What determines their values? What truths are the foundation for their attitudes? Where are they leading you?

"There are friends, boon companions, who will not be with you when sorrow comes." Who will you talk to when you become an alcoholic? Pregnant? Deprived of a God you know how to deal with? Without a faith to pass on to your children? When you realize your life is meaningless; empty? When your soul desires to soar?

"Faithful friends are a life-saving remedy; those who fear the Lord will find them." If you stay in bounds you will make friends with those you meet there. And vice-versa.

"Those who fear the Lord behave accordingly. And their friends will be like them." Like attracts like. If your standards are clear, you will bond with people who support them. This leads to "communion in the Holy Spirit."

"Guide me, Lord, in the way of your commands." He will, if we choose friends who will walk with us.

Meditation: Is my lifestyle different from that of my friends? Why is that?

February 26, 2011

Sirach 17:1-15; Psalm 103; Mark 10:13-16.

The Lord's kindness is everlasting to those who fear him.

Sirach 17:1-15 takes us "back to basics" to basic truths of life we never look at deeply. Or seldom think about.

"The Lord created humans out of earth, and in his own image he made them." We don't just exist. If we can see the hand in front of our face, we know it has nothing within itself to explain its existence. Nor does anything else in the universe. *Sirach* says we are "created." There is a self-explanatory Being whose existence is such that it needs no explanation. A Being who obviously, unimaginably just "is" by nature. And this is the name God gave himself: God said to Moses, "I AM WHO AM."[1]

We only exist because "HE WHO IS" gave and is giving us existence. Right now. He is saying, "Beeeee...." and holding the note. That makes the hand in front of our face intelligible.

"In his own image." We know we are like God because we can recognize his intention in the structure of things, "read his mind" in how different parts are related to each other. We can follow the Creator's thought process and praise him for it. Animals and atheists can't do this. Animals see that things work but not why. Engineers explain how things work, but stop there. They don't ask how they can *be*. Metaphysics (the "philosophy of being") explains that. Knowing the Being behind being, the

Person whose intention we recognize, makes *relationship* possible with the Creator. In this we discover ourselves.

God helps us do this, both through our natural power of intellect—*"he endowed humans with a strength of their own"*—and through revelation: *"With wisdom and knowledge he fills them... and shows them his glorious works, that they may describe the wonders of his deeds and praise his holy name."* We do this in the *Gloria* at Mass: "Lord God... we *worship* you, we *give you thanks*, we *praise* you for your glory."

The key is "fear of the Lord." This is not fright. Fear minus fright is *perspective*. We see what God is, compared to us, and we respect him. For Ben Sira, to keep this perspective in mind is the "beginning of wisdom" (1:1-20). Without it our understanding is reduced to groping and our will deprived of direction. There is no last end to orient us, nothing spiritual to appreciate.

To appreciate a principle, we have to live by what follows from it. *"If you desire wisdom, keep the commandments and the Lord will lavish her upon you, for the fear of the Lord is wisdom and discipline"* (1:26-27). A disordered life blocks truth. Obedience to God frees the mind from enslavement to blind appetites and cultural assumptions.

God can guide those who have a sense of perspective: *"Good and evil he shows them... he has set before them a law of life as their inheritance."* We echo that: *"The Lord's kindness is everlasting to those who fear him."*

[1] *Exodus 3:14.*

Meditation: How has "fear of the Lord" freed me to see and appreciate truth?

FOR REFLECTION AND DISCUSSION: WEEK SEVEN

The Seventh Week of Ordinary Time: The book of *Sirach*, also called *Ecclesiasticus*, invites us to reflect on creation, life, and relationship to God.

Invitation: To grow in desire for *wisdom* and commit ourselves to *discipleship*.

Ask yourself in prayer and others in discussion, for each statement below: Do you see this in the Scripture reading? What response does it invite?

Sirach 1:1-10: We need to seek wisdom where it can be found; in God's word.

The first step into discipleship is to declare yourself a learner through some visible form of concrete commitment.

Knowing I am committed to grow as a disciple is a mystical experience of call.

We don't realize we are committed until we don't feel like doing it any more.

Sirach 4:11-19: Those who want wisdom "*love life*," because they want to grow.

We win God's "favor" just by *desiring* to grow in wisdom.

Desire must pass into action. Perseverance is the true measure of desire.

Wisdom is "appreciation for spiritual things," and the "habit of relating everything to our last end."

Sirach 5:1-10: What makes meditation on Scripture "work" is a practical focus. If you don't get any great thoughts, just ask, How can I respond, what can I *do*?

Meditation requires us to make decisions with confidence, but depends on recognized powerlessness.

If we don't invest time in prayer, the rest of our time will be wasted.

Sirach 6:5-17: When we choose our friends, we are in fact choosing our way of life. Our choices are all influenced by the communal choices of our culture.

Like attracts like. If we live by our ideals we will bond with people who support them. This leads to "communion in the Holy Spirit."

Sirach 17:1-15: The basic truths are often the ones we seldom look at.

We know we are like God because we can recognize intention in the structure of things, follow the Creator's thought process and admire and praise him for it. Animals and atheists can't do this.

"Fear of the Lord" is fear minus fright; that is, *perspective*.

To appreciate a principle, we have to live by what follows from it. A disordered life blocks truth. Obedience to God frees the mind from enslavement to error.

Meditations:

Ask deeply and honestly, "Who is God for me?"
Do I truly want "wisdom"? Enough to become a committed disciple?
Is my lifestyle different from that of my friends? Why is that?
How has "fear of the Lord" freed me to see and appreciate truth?

FEBRUARY 27, 2011
In God Alone

INVENTORY

Are you ever anxious? Stressed out? Who isn't? But how do you deal with it? What is your response? (And how does it work for you?)

INPUT

The *Entrance Antiphon* gives the response God inspires: *"The Lord has been my strength."* But not just strength to endure: *"He has led me into freedom."* We can be free of stress and anxiety. The bottom line: *"He saved me because he loves me."* If he who is Power Itself, the Source and Sustainer of all existence, loves me and chooses to keep willing me into existence, even sharing his own divine life with me and uniting me to Jesus Christ as his body on earth, what do I have to worry about?

The *Opening Prayer* focuses us on the mystery of our true identity, which puts everything else into perspective: *"Form in us the likeness of your Son and deepen his life within us."* That life is "life to the full," eternal life. What more do we need?

It is true we are living in *"a world of fragile peace and broken promises."* But we aren't just "here." We are "sent" *"as witnesses of Gospel joy."* We have embraced our being-in-the-world voluntarily. For us it is not just a fact, it is a mission. We are here to take the initiative. We know the answer to all the world's problems: *"Touch the hearts of all people with your love, that they in turn may love one another."*

Is it that simple? Yes, it is.

SOMETHING TO COUNT ON

Isaiah 49:14-15 says it all. When did we feel most secure and at peace? In the womb? In our mother's arms as infants? Why?

First, we had nothing to do but be there. No tasks or goals to accomplish; no bills to pay or obligations to meet. We could just be. Secondly, we knew we were safe and loved.

The *Responsorial* (*Psalm* 62) encourages us to be this way with God: *"Rest in God alone, my soul."* Jesus said it too:

Martha was distracted by her many tasks.... But the Lord answered her, "Martha, Martha, you are worried and distracted by many things; there is need of only one thing."[1]

The rest of the *Responsorial Psalm* gives two reasons: *"From him comes my salvation.... From him comes my hope."* This is the answer both to fears and to desires; to anxieties about losing what we have and to fear of failure in what we want to do. God will save us from what threatens our existence: "he is my salvation." God will empower us to achieve our desires: "he is my hope." *Be at rest, my soul.* But *"only in God."* If we try to find security,

35

fulfillment, or peace in anything else, we will be disappointed. Jesus said, "Come to me, all you that are weary and are carrying heavy burdens, and I will give you rest." *"Only in God is my soul at rest."*[2]

"SEEK FIRST..." AND ONLY

Jesus says this again in **Matthew 6:24-34** and gets explicit about what we are not to worry about: the basics of survival: "your livelihood, what you are to eat or drink or use for clothing." Or, for that matter, even staying alive: "Which of you by worrying can add a moment to your lifespan?"

This could be just stoic resignation, which is elevated to a higher level in the "Serenity Prayer" that *Wikipedia* attributes to the theologian Reinhold Niebuhr. It was adopted by Alcoholics Anonymous and other twelve-step programs, and widely distributed by the U.S. Army to the distressed in Germany after World War II:

> God, grant me the serenity
> To accept the things I cannot change;
> Courage to change the things I can;
> And wisdom to know the difference.

Seen in a Christian context, this is more than stoic resignation to things we can do nothing about. And Jesus is far beyond this. He begins and ends with monotheism: that there is one God, and to let anything but God have any influence in our life is idolatry. "No one can serve two masters." This is the First Commandment: "I the LORD am your God... you shall not have other gods besides me."[3] Therefore, Jesus says, "Seek first [and only] his kingship over you, his way of holiness, and all these things will be given to you besides."

Stress is fragmentation. In single-minded dedication to the service of God we find the freedom and the unity of peace.

Jesus teaches that God is not just our Lord; he is our Father. We can and should count on him to provide for us with a Father's love. "Your heavenly Father knows all that you need."

To convince us, he points to two things we know: God provides for the birds that don't work, and for the flowers that die overnight; and we are more important to God than they are.[4]

Then he "zooms in" on what is more important in our own priorities: "Is not life more than food? Is not the body more valuable than clothes?" Jesus is saying, "If you keep yourself aware of God's priorities and of your own, you won't sweat the small stuff."

Compared to who God is and the work we are invited to do for God, everything else is "small stuff." It is the "unbelievers" who are "always running after" things like prosperity and success, status and security. We have only one goal to pursue: the holiness to be found in personal surrender to God, and the establishment of his reign over everything else on earth. They are one and the same: "So now, O Israel, what does the LORD your God require of you? Only to fear the LORD your God, to walk in all his ways, to love him, to serve the LORD your God with all your heart and with all your soul...."[5]

Jesus also teaches us to find the "peace of the present moment." He introduces the time factor: Why worry about tomorrow? "Let tomorrow take care of itself. Today has trouble enough of its own."

Again, this is not stoic resignation, even that acknowledged in Scripture as the attitude of those who do not know what God offers after death:

> Let us eat and drink,
> For tomorrow we die.[6]

Jesus is saying something developed later by the Jesuit Pierre de Caussade in his classic book, *Abandonment to Divine Providence*. The only thing we need be concerned with is doing God's will at the present moment. Period. And accepting whatever God is allowing to happen to us beyond our control at the present moment. We are not responsible today for what God wants us to do tomorrow (unless God's will today is that we should prepare for it). If right here and now we are doing what God wants us to do here and now, it is foolish to worry about anything else. This assumes, of course, that we are engaging now in any necessary discernment about decisions we must be prepared to face in the future. Just live in the present moment.

Jesus is situating our life between two poles: its beginning in God and its end in the Kingdom. If we are in union with Jesus as the Alpha and the Omega, we will live in peace.

> Christ yesterday and today,
> The beginning and the end,
> Alpha and Omega:
> All time belongs to him
> And all ages.
> To him be glory and power
> Through every age for ever.[7]

"YOUR TOIL IS NOT IN VAIN"

1Corinthians 4:1-5 gives the *coup de grace* to stress. We are "stewards of the mysteries of God." Our first concern is just to be "trustworthy," faithful to the Lord. Paul says, "The Lord is the one to judge me," so it "matters little" what anyone else thinks. We work only for God, and for others only in the measure and manner that we believe God desires. We don't have to please any boss but God. People may think what they want of us, but "at the time of his return" Jesus will "bring to light... the intentions of hearts." The name for this is freedom. *"Rest in God alone, my soul."*

[1]*Luke 10:40-42.*
[2]*Matthew 11:28.*
[3]*Deuteronomy 5:6-9.*
[4]Compare this to *Jonah 4:5-11.*
[5]*Deuteronomy 10:12.*
[6]See this presented stoically in *Ecclesiastes* (Quoheleth) 9:5-10 and *1Corinthians* 15:20-34; and with disapproval in *Wisdom* 2:8-9; *Isaiah 22:12-13.*
[7]Easter Vigil Mass: Blessing of the candle as a symbol of sanctifying all time.

INSIGHT:
Are you living for one thing or for many? Can the many be found in the one?

INITIATIVE:
Keep saying, "Lord, do this with me, do this in me, do this through me," and relax.

FEBRUARY 28, 2011

Sirach 17:19-27; Psalm 32; Mark 10:17-27.

Exult and rejoice in the Lord.

The fact is that, though blessed by God's light, we sometimes fail to walk in it. But for those with eyes to see, even our faults reveal God's goodness by giving us the experience of his mercy. **Sirach 17:19-27** assures us, *"To the penitent he provides a way back, he encourages those who are losing hope."*

Why does God make it so easy to return to him? Why doesn't he just give up on those who give up on him? We do.

We do because people can threaten us. We see them as able to diminish our happiness, take away what we think we need or want to keep. So when people threaten to do us harm, we want to exclude them from our lives, ostracize them, lock them away in cages, even execute or exterminate them. This is because we recognize our existence as fragile, incomplete, and tenuous. We are fixated on protecting it.

Not so God. God doesn't protect his life; he shares it. God doesn't have to defend his existence; he gives existence to all that is. God sees everything from a different perspective.

> *How great is the mercy of the Lord, his forgiveness to those who return to Him! The like cannot be found in humans, for not immortal is any child of man.*

Ben Sira is not denying the immortality of the soul, although in his time the Jews may not have known much about it. That is not his question or focus. What he is pointing out is that God relates to people from a different perspective than ours. Even though we are in God's image he is infinitely better. God's only concern is to help every person to grow to the fullness of life. God is pure giving because there is nothing he needs to receive or defend. God is not afraid of losing anything, because he has everything.

Except our total surrender to his love. God doesn't "possess" our free will. He won't force it. He wants to win it. But he knows the only way to win love freely is to give love unconditionally.

So no matter what we do to him he responds with love. No matter where we stand in relationship to him: near or far, thinking we are in favor or in disgrace, *"Return to the Lord, give up sin, pray to him and make your offenses few."*

Few. Diminish them. We don't have to be perfect overnight, wholehearted in our first response. *"Turn again to the Most High and away from sin."* Turn. It's a matter of direction, of fundamental desire, of mind-set. Just accept the goal and start. Life is a journey. So is love.

This is the first call of the Good News. "In those days John the Baptizer appeared in the wilderness of Judea, proclaiming, 'Repent, for the kingdom of heaven has come near'.... Jesus began to proclaim, 'Repent, for the kingdom of heaven has come near.'" *Metanoieite!* Change your minds and hearts. New life is at hand. Accept it.[1]

To live a new life, we need to accept a new guidance system. God's. We need to let his words, not our assumptions, direct our course. Be disciples.

[1] *Matthew 3:2; 4:17.*

Meditation: Which direction am I facing? Do I need to alter course at all?

MARCH 1, 2011

Sirach 35:1-12; Psalm 50; Mark 10:28-31.

To the upright I will show the saving power of God.

Most religions include some kind of conscious giving to God. Ritual sacrifices. Support of the poor or of what we recognize as "God's work." But **Sirach 35:1-12** says the first of all gifts is to *"keep the law."* This is a *"great oblation."*

We have to give something. *"Appear not before the Lord empty-handed."* But what gives value to the gift is the attitude of the giver. What God sees in our hands is the expression of our heart. We can't "buy God." *"Offer no bribes, these he does not accept."* God does not want our gifts but our giving; that is, he wants us. And he wants us loving, because when we love we are like God, which is what we were created to be.

That is why in giving, attitude counts more than the content. Giving is an act of relationship. If we don't give with a sincere desire to be in the right relationship with God (and with others) our giving is pleasing to no one. To "have mercy" is to "come to the aid of another out of a sense of *relationship.*" Christian giving is not condescension; it is *recognition:* we recognize God as God and Father, our brother as brother, our sister as sister. Christian giving is always family support.

We have to give like God: *"in a generous spirit... in a spirit of joy.... Give to the Most High as he has given to you, generously, according to your means."*

God gives All. All he is, and all he has made he offers to us. And he asks for all in return. "You shall love the LORD your God with *all* your heart, and with *all* your soul, and with *all* your might." This is what Jesus recognized and praised in the "widow's mite":

> Truly I tell you, this poor widow has put in more than all those who are contributing to the treasury. For all of them have contributed out of their abundance; but she out of her poverty has put in everything she had, all she had to live on.[1]

All. "Sin" is mentioned in the Bible 367 times. "All" appears 4491 times. "Love" 491 times. Jesus demanded all for All:

> The kingdom of heaven is like treasure hidden in a field, which someone found and... in joy goes and sells all and buys that field. None of you can become my disciple if you do not give up all your possessions.[2]

We can't out-give God. *"For the Lord is one who always repays, and he will give back to you sevenfold,"* that is, in perfect measure.[3] Jesus said the same:

> Give, and it will be given to you. A good measure, pressed down, shaken together, running over, will be put into your lap; for the measure you give will be the measure you get back.

The measure is proportional, not equal. God's measure is exponentially higher than ours. People who trust in God's generosity will discover how great it is. *To the upright I will show the saving power of God.*

[1] *Deuteronomy* 6:5; *Mark* 12:43-44.
[2] *Matthew* 13:44-46; *Luke* 14:33;
[3] For the significance of "seven" see Monday of Week Six above, February 14.

Meditation: What am I giving to God? Do I give in the same spirit God does?

MARCH 2, 2011

Sirach 36:1-17; Psalm 79; Mark 10:32-45.

Show us, O Lord, the light of your kindness.

The liturgy omits verses 6-9 in this reading for an obvious reason. They ask God to crush Israel's enemies, while in the *Responsorial* Psalm we ask God, *"Show us the light of your kindness."*

The liturgy is telling us not to see in **Sirach 36:1-17** an approbation of vengeance and violence. Ben Sira saw these as a means to convince people of God's power and fidelity to Israel—a common error, then and now. We still pray, "Show us you love us; hurt our enemies." But this is not Sirach's point.

God didn't try to correct all the cultural assumptions of his People. It would take the crucifixion and resurrection of Jesus to do that. Until then, even Christ's chosen apostles rejected God's way of saving the world. (See *Matthew* 16:21-28). So God inspired Ben Sira to write according to the way he and others thought, but the liturgy identifies the point God was making as distinct from its cultural dressing. Ben Sira was asking God to make manifest his fidelity and kindness to Israel so that all people on earth would know, *"there is no God but you."* The passage ends: *"Thus it will be known to the very ends of the earth that you are the eternal God."*

Jesus revealed this as the first priority of his own heart when he taught us to pray, "Our Father... *hallowed be thy name!*" This should be our first priority and greatest desire in everything we do.

Jesus' second priority is the means to this: *"Thy Kingdom come!"* The world appreciates God as God when the reign of his love is established in every heart. This is Ben Sira's thinking:

> Gather all the tribes of Jacob... Show mercy to the people called by your name.... with your glory.

We pray and try to live in such a way that God's reigning presence will be visible in his Church. *"Give evidence of your deeds of old."* We ask that the fervor of the saints and martyrs, the miracles of faith and conversion that characterized the Church in its beginning will be visible in our day as they have been in every age since Christianity began. *"Let your prophets be proved true"*—those of every generation who called the Church to fidelity, and those in our time who are calling for a "new evangelization."

To evangelize, the Church must make visible God's reign in herself: in every individual and Church institution. The "fruit of the Spirit" must manifest the presence of the Spirit in all we do.

We can make this happen if we 1. make conscious, intimate, personal relationship (interaction) with Jesus Christ the core of all we do; 2. "devote ourselves to the apostles' teaching" as *disciples*; 3. bear *witness* as *prophets* through the radical "differentness" of our lifestyle; 4. minister to each other as a community of *priests* in "fellowship, the breaking of bread and the prayers" (see *Acts* 2:42); 5. take responsibility for changing the Church and society as *stewards* of Christ's kingship. The world is asking us: *"Show us, Christians, the light of your kindness."*

Meditation: Do I live to make God known? Can I live in a way that will?

MARCH 3, 2011

Sirach 42:15-25; Psalm 33; Mark 10:46-52.

By the word of the Lord the heavens were made.

Sirach 42:15-25 is a meditation on what *Genesis* told us about creation: *"Now will I recall God's works; what I have seen, I will describe."*

The first act of meditation is to use our *memory* to "recall" a truth. In this St. Catherine of Siena says we are like God the Father who said, "Let it be" and it was. By memory we can "make present" in our mind what we will.

The second step is to use *intellect* to "describe" what we see, look at it more closely, explore its dimensions, bring out what may not be noticed at first glance. In using *intellect* we discover our likeness to God the Son: the *Word*, the very intelligibility (*Logos*) of God. All creation is intelligible, because every creature is a work of God who is Intelligibility itself. Ben Sira recognizes beings as embodying God's "word":

> At God's word were his works brought into being; they do his will as he has ordained for them.

When we recognize the intelligibility of beings, our minds are "echoing" the creative process of God who designed them. We experience our likeness to the *Logos* who has ordered the universe.

St. Paul's reflection on this brings us into the deep mystery of Jesus:

> For in him all things in heaven and on earth were created, things visible and invisible... all things have been created through him and for him. He himself is before all things, and in him all things hold together.[1]

Sirach tells us everyone can see enough to admire and praise God: *"As the rising son is clear to all, so the glory of the Lord fills all his works."*

But we know we see only the tip of the iceberg. *"Yet even God's holy ones must fail in recounting the wonders of the Lord."* There is always more.

This leads Ben Sira to stand in awe before the "breadth and length and height and depth" of God's knowledge:

> He plumbs the depths and penetrates the heart; their innermost being he understands. The Most High possesses all knowledge... the past and the future.... Perennial is his almighty wisdom; he is from all eternity one and the same....

The third step in meditation is to use our *wills* to love and rejoice in the unity of Goodness and Truth we see reflecting the union of Father and Son in Creation. In this we experience our likeness to the Holy Spirit, the personification of response to the mutual knowledge and love between Father and Son.

This is the progress of wisdom: from 1. seeing the world to 2. seeing it as the work of God, to 3. seeing the mystery of God himself. Then back to the world, seen through what we know of God. If God is all good and wise, then all God made must be good and created for a reason:

> How beautiful are all his works!... All of them differ... yet none of them has he made in vain. For each... is good. Can one ever see enough of their splendor?

With the Spirit we respond, affirming in bonding appreciation, *"By the word of the Lord the heavens were made."*

[1] *John* 1:1-18; 14:6; *Colossians* 1:16-17.

Meditation: Do I see God in the world, the world in God, and myself in both?

41

MARCH 4, 2011

Sirach 44:1-13; Psalm 149; Mark 11:11-26.

The Lord takes delight in his people.

Sirach 44:1-13 mentions categories of people "glorious in their time" who "left behind a name," and people still talk about their great deeds. *"But of others,"* he says, *"there is no memory. When they ceased they ceased."* Period. *"Yet these also were godly persons,"* Ben Sira says, *"whose virtues have not been forgotten."* These are the ones *Sirach* deals with.

The Jews at that time were not too clear about life after death. There was not much to look forward to after you died. *Sheol*, the "abode of the dead" (sometimes translated *Hades*), was not a desirable place to be. God rewarded those who were pleasing to him by giving them a long, full life on earth. But *Sirach* gives another perspective.[1]

Ben Sira had said about those who are not famous for anything that, when they die *"they are as though they had not lived."* Now he reverses that.

> *Their wealth remains in their families,*
> *their heritage is with their descendants.*

This could be taken to mean just that they passed on their property to their children as an inheritance. Or we could say it means the real wealth of their own lives, and what they have to show for them, is found precisely in their children. Descendants are not just one's heirs; they are the heritage one leaves to the human race. *"In their descendants they find a rich inheritance, their posterity."*

Translations differ. The next line reads either: *"Through God's covenant with them their family endures,"* or *"Their descendants stand by the covenants [or commandments] and, thanks to them, so do their children's children."*[2]

Whether we say families survive as a result of God's promise, or that those who live in union with God will be able to pass their faith on to their children, *Sirach* concludes: *"For all time their progeny will endure, their glory will never be blotted out."* That is something to live for.

This is still valid reasoning, even though we believe in "heaven," an eternal life of beatific union with God as the reward of persevering in grace. It is true that Christians don't *need* children and grandchildren in order to "live on" in this world after death. Our true—and promised—"posterity" is in those whom we have helped to accept the divine life of grace or to grow in it. St. Paul saw ministry as bringing Christ to birth and to "full stature" in others.[3]

Still, we should not let the better blind us to the good. In family is fulfillment. Parents last longer than presidents. And do more good. Better to write God's name on one child's heart than to be besieged for autographs. And better to fill children's minds with wisdom than book-racks with best sellers. We believe *"The Lord takes delight in his people."* All of them.

[1]On the other hand, see *Daniel* 12:1-3 and *2Maccabees* 7:9, 23, 29, from the same period.
[2]Compare the *New American*, the *New Revised Standard*, and the *New Jerusalem* Bibles.
[3]*1Corinthians* 4:14-15; *Galatians* 4:19; *Ephesians* 4:11-16.

Meditation: What do I want to "leave behind" when I die? Is it the best of me?

MARCH 5, 2011

Sirach 51:12-20; Psalm 19; Mark 11:27-33.

The precepts of the Lord give joy to the heart.

Sirach 51:12-20 could be called a *Hymn to Discipleship*. If you weren't sure you wanted to pursue wisdom before, Ben Sira's testimony, telling his experience, should convince you!

1. Wisdom gives saving *relationship*. "My feet kept to the level path *because from earliest youth I was familiar with her.*" He knows he gained through *interaction* with a Person. "Since in this way I have profited, *I will give my teacher grateful praise.*" For us, the Teacher is Jesus, Wisdom Incarnate. To be *Christian* is to cultivate *relationship* with him through deep, conscious, personal interaction.

2. Wisdom stimulates committed *discipleship*. "*I became resolutely devoted to her... never turning back.*" The more we learn of the mind and heart of God, the more we want to learn.

3. Wisdom inspires, because she requires purification. "*For her I purified my hands; in cleanness I attained to her.*" Wisdom calls us beyond simple law-observance to stricter conduct based on *prophetic* insight. When we have the courage to "*open her gate,*" in personal decisions that take us "out of the box" of enclosing laws and customs, we will "*come to know her secrets.*" Wisdom is a school of discernment, which requires detachment from other desires.

4. Wisdom leads to surrender to God and ministry to others. There comes a time when we know we have "*gained understanding*" and that wisdom has become our "*prize possession.*" But not through achievement. Through surrender. What we "possess," we possess by being united to Christ in habitual surrender to his will, his guidance, his inspirations. Because of this, Christ can *express* himself freely through our physical words and actions to give life to others. "*The Lord has granted me my lips as a reward*"— freed me from inhibiting fear and reserve—"*and my tongue will declare his praise.*" Now we minister to others as sharing in Christ's *priesthood*. Ben Sira offers to minister by teaching all who desire wisdom: "*Come aside to me, you untutored, and take up lodging in the house of instruction.*" Wisdom shared gives blessings both ways.

5. Wisdom empowers perseverance through promise. Ben Sira's poem promises that wisdom is "close to those who seek her." She will give herself and all her blessings to those who persevere: "*The one who is in earnest finds her.*" We need to "*submit our neck to her yoke*" without reserves and abandon ourselves to pursuing her without looking back.[1] And without setting time limits. For *perseverance* we draw on the same spirit of hope and anticipation of reward as those *faithful stewards* who are working to establish Christ's kingdom until he comes again. *Sirach's* final words are: "*Work at your tasks in due season, and in his own time God will give you his reward.*"[2]

[1]See *Luke* 9:62; *1Kings* 19:19-21.
[2]Numbers 4 and 5 are from verses 21-30.

Meditation: Am I sold on pursuing wisdom? Why? How can I do it?

43

FOR REFLECTION AND DISCUSSION: WEEK EIGHT

The Eighth Week of Ordinary Time: The readings show us how to reflect on creation and life to discover God's mercy, priorities, generosity. They call us to make God visible in ourselves; to recognize our likeness to Father, Son, and Spirit.

They identify fulfillment for the non-famous and list five benefits Wisdom gives.

Invitation: To confirm our desire to seek *wisdom* through committed *discipleship*.

Ask yourself in prayer and others in discussion, for each statement below: Do you see this in the Scripture reading? What response does it invite?

Sirach 17:19-27: Our faults show us God's goodness by revealing his mercy.

We want to exclude or execute people who do us harm, because we are fixated on protecting our fragile existence. God, above fear, responds to everything with love.

God wins people to love freely by giving love unconditionally.

In our response to God, what counts is direction, fundamental desire. We don't have to be wholehearted; just accept the goal and start. Life is a journey. So is love.

Sirach 35:1-12: The first of all gifts to God is to "*keep the law*" in its full sense. Gifts to God are measured by intention, not volume. The attitude of the giver gives value to the gift. God sees in our hands the expression of our heart.

Christian giving is an act of *recognition*: of *relationship* with God and others.

Sirach 36:1-17: God does not show his fidelity and kindness to us by vengeance against our enemies. We are to pray, work, and live in such a way that God's reigning presence will be visible in his Church.

Sirach 42:15-25: The *Genesis* account of creation tells us: 1. By *memory* we are like God the Father. 2. By *intellect* we are like God the Son as Word (*Logos*). 3. By *will* we are like the Holy Spirit.

Sirach 44:1-13: Tells us unsung people "make history" by living on in their children, especially those who persevere in faith and fidelity to the covenant.

Sirach 51:12-20: Motives to embrace discipleship are that Wisdom:
1. introduces us to personal *relationship* with God; 2. motivates and guides committed *discipleship*; 3. stimulates purification for bearing *witness* as *prophets*; 4. leads to surrender and union with God in *ministry* as *priests*; 5. gives promises that encourage *perseverance* as *stewards*.

Meditations:

Which direction am I facing? Do I need to alter course at all?
What am I giving to God? Do I give in the same spirit God does?
Do I live to make God known? Can I live in a way that will?
Do I see God in the world, the world in God, and myself in both?
What do I want to "leave behind" when I die? Is it what is best in me?
Am I sold on pursuing wisdom? Why? How can I do it?

MARCH 6, 2011

A Fundamental Choice

INVENTORY

What are you most afraid of? Do you believe and trust that God can and will protect you from this? Do you know what you need to do to receive God's help?

INPUT

The liturgy calls our attention to fundamentals. This Sunday's *Opening Prayer* focuses on our need to have God protect and provide for us: "Keep us from danger and provide for all our needs." The Latin actually asks for "all that will be of benefit to us," which may include some things we don't think we need and exclude others we do. The *Alternate Opening Prayer* tells us how God does that, and what we need to do to receive his help. God does it through his "gifts." To be able to receive them we ask God: "Teach us to cherish [love].... Increase our faith... Bring our trust [hope] to its promised fulfillment." Our greatest need, whether we are aware of it or not, is for faith, hope, and love. The *Prayer Over the Gifts* develops this: "Make us holy by sharing your life with us." Do we feel that as our greatest need? The *Prayer After Communion* asks, "Guide us with your Spirit." It presumes we want to "honor" God, "not only with our lips but also with the lives we lead." And why? So that we might "enter your kingdom." You can't get more fundamental than this.

LIFE IS AN EITHER-OR

Deuteronomy 11:18-32 tells us our life can be a blessing or a curse. And it's our choice. "A blessing for obeying the commandments of the Lord, your God... a curse if you do not obey." This says three things.

1. Nothing makes life a blessing or curse but our free choice. Neither depends on health, wealth, success, circumstances, or what others do for us or to us. To think so is to live under a fundamental illusion that can be the greatest mistake of our lives.

2. God says—and he knows something about it!—that if we live by his words we will be happy. And if we don't we won't. His commandments "keep us from danger" and teach us a way of life in which God can "provide for all our needs." Take it or leave it.

3. God protects us and provides for us through the gift of *revelation*— through the words he has spoken and continues to speak to every person who reads them in Scripture. This is what we believe as Church: "In the sacred books the Father who is in heaven *meets his children* with great love and *speaks with them.*" Jesus said it clearly: "I am the way, and the truth, and the life." If we study his truth and follow his way, we will experience his life. But we have to express our faith, "not only with our lips but also with the lives we lead."[1]

This, in a nutshell, says, "Be disciples!" Be *students* of the mind and heart of God—the source of all his commandments—by reading and reflecting on his words. In real life, in practice, the choice to make one's life a "blessing" or a "curse," comes down to the very specific and concrete decision "to be or not to be" a *disciple*. And we have to make that decision, "not only with our lips but also with the lives we lead." Being a disciple means doing something; something down-to-earth and daily, like putting a Bible on the pillow where we will have to pick it up at least once a day, and beginning to actually read it. God says in the reading, *"Take these words of mine into your heart and soul. Teach them to your children, talking about them when you are at home and when you are away, when you lie down and when you rise."*

We will or we won't. Our choice.

In **Matthew 7:21-27** Jesus emphasizes the words of the *Prayer After Communion*: "also with the lives we lead."

First he establishes the need to become *disciples*: "students" of his words. It is not enough just to accept him as our Savior and Lord. "Not everyone who says to me, 'Lord, Lord,' will enter the kingdom of heaven, but only the one who does the will of my Father."

To really know God's will we have to study his words—all our life long. St. Paul makes clear what we committed ourselves to at Baptism: "Do not be conformed to this world, but be *transformed by the renewing of your minds*, so that *you may discern* what is the will of God—what is good and acceptable and perfect." The Church says it just as clearly in the *Rite of Christian Initiation of Adults*: "If, then, you wish to become his disciples and members of his Church, you must be guided to the *fullness of the truth* that he has revealed to us. You must learn to *make the mind of Christ Jesus your own*. You must strive to *pattern your life on the teachings of the Gospel....*"[2]

"Dead fish float downstream; live fish swim upstream." This proverb describes the Church: those who just float with the current—even the Catholic current—doing what everyone else does, are "dead." Not absolutely; they are not in "mortal sin." Even the smattering of discipleship we got in religion classes and still get weekly during the *Liturgy of the Word* at Mass is enough, perhaps, to make our lives more of a blessing than a curse—just not enough to make them the blessing, to ourselves and others, that God wants them to be. Being a lockstep Catholic, professing all the doctrines, keeping all the rules, and following all the practices, is a good conformism, but it is still just conformism. And conformists are the "walking dead." They make Christianity a "religion" that is not at the same time a "spirituality"—one reason the young give for turning away from it to seek "enlightenment" in Hinduism, Buddhism, or other non-Christian traditions. They make us think of God's words to the good but mediocre bishop (or church) of Laodicea:

> I know your works; you are neither cold nor hot. I wish that you were either cold or hot. So, because you are lukewarm... I am about to spit you out of my mouth.[3]

Whether they are "spit out" or simply splitting, Catholics are leaving the Church at a rate that recalls the Protestant Reformation. And often for the same reason: they are looking for a "more" that is, in fact, available in the Church—in overwhelming measure—but which they never found because they were just following the crowd that comes to church and goes home without it making much of an impact on them. They discover, somehow, another group that is actively exploring the word of God and they come alive as if they had discovered a new world.

The fault here lies both with them and with the effectiveness of our pastoral ministry.

Jesus continues: "Anyone who hears my words and does not put them into practice" is building a house on sand. That person's religion will collapse.

Romans 3:21-28 tells us what the working element is in discipleship. Its effectiveness does not depend on how much time we give to reflecting on God's word, or even how much effort we put into living it out — though both of these are essential. What really makes discipleship "work" is *faith.*

Discipleship is not essentially study. Or if it is, that study is defined as *"faith seeking understanding"* (the traditional definition of "theology"). Discipleship is a process of letting the divine gift of God—faith—"take flesh" in human words and actions. We "translate" the word of God into words that our intellects can comprehend (though never perfectly). We apply those words to our own lives, asking how we can embody them in the kind of actions they call for in our time and place and circumstances.

This is not just "self-help" or some kind of intellectual exercise. It is a quest for the enlightenment that only God can give, and as we seek light we ask for light. It is a gift.

[1]Vatican II: "Liturgy," no. 33; *John* 14:6.
[2]*Romans* 12:1-2; Candidates' First Acceptance of the Gospel, no. 52 C.
[3]*Revelation* 3:14-19.

INSIGHT:
What does it take for you to say with confidence, "O Lord, be my rock of safety"?

INITIATIVE:
Make a choice that will make you a disciple.

MARCH 7, 2011

Tobit 1:3 to 2:8; Psalm 112; Mark 12:1-12.

Happy the one who fears the Lord.

The liturgy has us read the *Book of Tobit* on all the weekdays of Week Nine. Its goal is to teach wisdom through the fascinating story that it tells.

Tobit 1:3 to 2:8 introduces Tobit as a Jewish exile who is an example of fidelity to the law. Tobit is not boasting when he says of himself: "I have walked all the days of my life on the paths of truth and righteousness." He is simply making a profession of faith and of loyalty to God and to the religion of his people. He continued to perform the authentic rituals of Israel, he says, even when "all of my kinsmen, like the rest of the tribe," succumbed to cultural pressure: "I would often make the pilgrimage alone to Jerusalem for the festivals.... All my brothers and relatives ate the food of heathens, but I refrained...."

He didn't just stand up against the laxity of his family and fellow Jews. He also broke the law by burying executed Israelites, which was forbidden under pain of death. When he fled into hiding, all his property was confiscated. And when he returned under a different ruler, he did it again. His neighbors called him a fool: "Will this man never learn?" But the question the story confronts us with is, "Will *we* ever learn?"

We don't think of ourselves as exiles deported to a foreign land hostile to our religion. We don't see ourselves as a tiny minority immersed in a pagan culture.

That is because we have done spiritually what Tobit did physically: we have closed our eyes and gone to sleep, heedless of our environment. And what happened to Tobit (as we will see tomorrow) happened to us. While we slept we were blinded.

Thomas Jefferson is credited with saying, "The price of liberty is eternal vigilance." If we take for granted we are free, we will one day discover we are slaves—if by that time we are not too blind to see it. The truth is, we are in "enemy territory." Every Christian is. Always and everywhere. The United States is a foreign land for us, one that follows and draws us to follow an unenlightened culture—a culture Pope John Paul II characterized as being in some respects a "culture of death." The same is true of every country and culture on earth. This world, as centuries of human sins and errors have distorted it, is simply not a place where Christians can be at home. Peter calls us "aliens and exiles" here. Paul reminds us "our citizenship is in heaven."

> You are a chosen race, a royal priesthood, a holy nation, God's own people, in order that you may proclaim the mighty acts of him who called you out of darkness into his marvelous light.... Conduct yourselves honorably among the Gentiles, so that, though they malign you as evildoers, they may see your honorable deeds and glorify God when he comes to judge.[1]

We need to scrutinize and question every trend, every goal, every priority our culture draws us into. What is good we accept; but we don't accept anything as good without discernment.

[1] *1 Peter* 2:9-12; *Philippians* 3:20.

Meditation: How am I different from a "good American"? What do I question?

MARCH 8, 2011

Tobit 2:9-14; Psalm 112; Mark 12:13-17.

The heart of the just person is secure, trusting in the Lord.

We would think someone as faithful to God as Tobit would enjoy the happy life Scripture keeps promising to those who live by God's law. But he is hit with one disaster after another. He loses his property, his eyesight, the approval of his neighbors, and seems to lose even the respect of his wife. It afflicts him so much that in the next chapter he will pray for death! Is this the fruit of wisdom? The fruit of keeping the law?

Tobit's wife turned on him because he was so afraid of being dishonest he accused her of stealing a goat that was given as a gift. Any married man could have told him, "Tobit, that wasn't smart." But the point of the story is not his suspicion, but his solicitude for keeping God's law. He did not let poverty compromise his fidelity to God.

In this instance, what it got him was a scathing reproach from his wife: "Where are your charitable deeds now... your virtuous acts? Your true character is finally showing itself!"

Admittedly, she had cause to be angry. But the story alerts us to a fact of life: when someone is more virtuous than others, they will jump on any failing to discount all the good they have seen up to then. We see it in people's reaction to scandals in the Church; whether horrible things like child abuse by a "minority of the minority" that is the clergy, or just the mediocrity of those who should be "models to the flock."

The failings of the clergy are glaringly public. But any Christian who refuses to conform to the culture and lives by the true spirit of Christ will be subject to the same unforgiving scrutiny. Any fault will serve as an excuse to discount all the good the Church does: help to the poor (in the United States, second only to the aid government gives); consistent participation and leadership in efforts for social justice; the heroism of countless "workplace" missionaries and martyrs, past and present (and those in foreign missions as well); a richness of doctrine that, though distorted at times, is full of challenge, balance, and mystery inviting "endless exploration," summoning us to strive for the "breadth and length and height and depth, and to know the love of Christ that surpasses knowledge," so that we may be "filled with all the fullness of God."[1]

Tobit got flak from his wife. All of us get it from anyone who is threatened by the ideals we proclaim or—more threateningly—live. So is it true that if we live by God's words we will be happy, and if we don't we won't?

Yes, it is true. But happiness does not exclude suffering and times of deep discouragement, even depression. Still:

> God is faithful, and he will not let you be tested beyond your strength, but... will also provide the way out so that you may be able to endure it.[2]

The heart of the just person is secure, trusting in the Lord.

[1] *Ephesians* 3:18-19.
[2] *1Corinthians* 10:13.

Meditation: Can I accept goodness that isn't perfect? In myself and others?

MARCH 9, 2011

Lent is a time to change together

INVENTORY

Do you think things can be turned around in our society without a massive conversion? Do you believe it will really help the world situation significantly if you yourself begin living more authentically? Is this the point of Lent?

INPUT

The readings summon us as individuals to convert as a community.

Joel 2:12-18 is addressed to the whole People of Israel as a community; not just to individuals who see themselves acting independently of others. No one corrupted our society independently of others. And no one will reform it independently of others. Lent is a time to hear the word of God together and respond to it as a community.

It is not true to say that if we don't act together, we should not act at all. But when we act as individuals in the Church (or in the human race!) we should do it in a way that will draw others to act with us. In spite of the fiction, the Lone Ranger is not nearly as effective as a posse. The word "posse" (Latin) means "to be able." Anything we accomplish "alone and unaided" we recognize as exceptional.

Lent, then, is a celebrated season that calls for a *communal* response.

When Joel said: "Proclaim a fast, call an assembly; gather the people, notify the congregation," he was talking to the whole People of Israel. To whom should we address this call today? To individuals? Parishes? Dioceses? Just the Catholic Church? All Christians? The whole world?

Matthew 6:1-18 sounds like a contradiction of what we have just said about com-

munal response. Jesus is saying the first thing we have to convert *from* is *religion*, and the first thing we have to convert *to* is *spirituality*. "Religion" as used here corresponds to what people mean when they speak disparagingly of "organized religion." It is not really organization they oppose (even the most private, individual life must be organized to be effective), but a system of organized external observances without interior ordination to God. Since what is interior is, by definition, individual, personal, and private, Jesus seems to be summoning us to convert to acting as individuals rather than as a community. That is not what he means.

The watchword for Christian authenticity is "both-and" as opposed to "either-or." There are some "either-or's"—the fundamental choice of the "blessing" or the "curse": life or death; to live or not live by the law of God; to remain in the darkness or be led into the light. But the big errors in living out the religion of "God-made-human" come when we think we have to be *either* divine or human; either physical or spiritual; either obedient or free; either surrendered to faith or guided by reason; either reliant on God or responsible for taking initiatives— and, either a Catholic or a Baptist! (Or Presbyterian or Methodist, etc.) But is it possible to be both? The correct answer to all the choices proposed above is "both-and."

The last example was included for shock value. But think about it. The Baptists say they don't know who is a Baptist. They accept anyone who is "saved." They might not have *fellowship* with someone they disagree with, but they claim no authority to declare anyone's interpretation of Scripture wrong. So there is no contradiction in a Baptist who interprets Scripture the way the Catholics do and joins the Church as *both* a "Baptist Catholic" *and* a "Catholic Baptist," living by the best in both traditions. (For example, participating in Mass on Sunday but singing the hymns and putting twice as much in the collection!)

Why shouldn't Catholics as well claim "double citizenship" through fellowship with any church that does not ask them to deny anything they believe, affirm anything they don't believe, or stop doing anything the Catholic Church requires? As long as fellowship is "both-and" it does not have to be "either-or."

There is a new surge among Christians toward unity. Catholics and Protestants often find themselves participating in each other's services. The question arises about Communion.

In practice we do what the bishop or pastor decides. But we need to ask what options there are in theory. Laws are always to be obeyed, but always according to the intention of the lawgiver. And we have to understand that intention in the light of our faith.

Catholics believe that "grace" is the *favor of sharing in the divine life of God.* The principal acts of grace—divine faith,

hope, and love—are in reality acts of sharing in God's own activity. By faith, for example, we share in God's own act of knowing.

Because we are both divine and human, our interior, divine act of sharing in God's knowledge might "take flesh" in human concepts and words that do not perfectly agree with the truth we possess in faith. What we possess may differ from what we profess. Examples:

The Magi were "saved" by believing in *whatever* the star God sent was leading them to. "Where is he?" they said to Herod: "We have come," not to "check him out," but "to adore him." They already adored Jesus Christ, and knew him as God, before they ever met him. This is classical "Baptism of desire."

Scripture scholars tell us the disciples believed in Jesus long before, through the Resurrection and Pentecost, they were able to recognize him as God. But if they knew him by faith, then interiorly they already knew him as God, whether or not they could have said this in words.

Did Jesus know he was God? Of course he did. From his birth:

> he has to be the Son of God and he has to know it…. But it is not necessary—and it is hardly probable—that this fundamental experience should from the beginning have taken the form of an intellectual certitude, of a clear concept.

In other words, as divine made human he always knew he was God. But as a human who was divine he could not always have said that in human words.[1]

Do saved Baptists, who by grace share in God's own knowing act through faith, but who stoutly assert that the bread and wine of Communion are nothing more than a symbol of fellowship, really know and believe, without being conscious of it, that they are in fact the Body and Blood of Christ? If we are consistent with our theology of grace, we have to say they do!

Also, by our theology of "Baptism of desire," if they believe unconditionally in the Bible and everything God intends to reveal through it, then they believe what the Bible really says about Eucharist—whether or not their human understanding, distorted by the controversies of the Reformation, allows them to express it in the right words. For any good Baptist, the actual truth of the Bible takes priority over any intellectual formulation of that truth, including their own. Whatever God means to say in the Bible, they believe it.

So logically, we Catholics, who know the Bible means that the bread and wine become the real Body and Blood of Christ, have to accept that the Baptists believe this too—whether they know it or not!

The Baptists may be Catholic after all! Where does this lead us?

2Corinthians 5:20 to 6:2: "We are ambassadors for Christ, God, as it were, appealing through us"—calling the whole world to turn around together. Is it time we broadened our ministry to address everyone who will listen? Time to open our doors to everyone we recognize as having "become Christ" through Baptism? Is it time Catholics and Protestants applied to themselves what Paul applied to Jews and Gentiles:

Now in Christ Jesus you who once were far off have been brought near by the blood of Christ.... In his flesh he has made both groups into one and has broken down the dividing wall, the hostility between us.

He has abolished the law with its commandments and ordinances, that he might create in himself one new humanity in place of the two, thus making peace, and might reconcile both groups to God in one body.... for through him both of us have access in one Spirit to the Father.

So then you are no longer strangers and aliens, but citizens with the saints and also members of the household of God....

Perhaps we could make this our principle focus as we recite the *Responsorial* (*Psalm 51*): "Be merciful O Lord, for we have sinned."

[1]Jacques Guillet, S.J., *The Consciousness of Jesus*, Newman, 1972, pp. 43-44.

INSIGHT:
Is Lent a "Catholic" season, or one we share with everyone?

INITIATIVE:
Participate in both Catholic and Protestant Lenten observances—preferably with the same people.

MARCH 10, 2011

Happy are they who hope in the Lord!
(Psalm 1).

Deuteronomy 30:15-20 sets before us the basic "either-or" choice of human existence: life and well-being or death and misery. God's gift; our choice. "Life or death, the blessing or the curse." All we have to do is accept it.

How do we know we have? Three times the reading describes acceptance as *listening*. To choose life is to "obey" (from *obaudire*, to "listen to"). It is "heeding God's voice." Those who refuse "will not listen." Obviously, to choose life means we choose to become *disciples*, "learners," people who *listen* to God's word in order to *learn*. This is the choice to keep learning from Jesus all our life; to keep reading and reflecting on his words and actions. Either we do or we don't. Our choice.

In *Acts*, those who accepted the Good News "*devoted themselves* to the apostles' teaching and fellowship, to the breaking of bread and the prayers." That is discipleship.[1]

Learning is sometimes described as a "change of behavior." That is only one aspect of it, of course, but it is true that any learning that does not affect the way we live or help us to live better— for example, by enhancing our appreciation of truth and beauty— is useless. In John's Gospel Jesus is presented as "Light" and "Life" interchangeably.

> In him was life, and the life was the light of all people.
> Jesus said, "I am the light of the world. Whoever follows me will never walk in darkness but will have the light of life.[2]

Discipleship is learning for living. In the reading, we "listen" to "obey the commandments of the Lord." "Heeding God's voice" entails "holding fast to him." Not to listen is to "turn away" our hearts and be "led astray." Discipleship is like eating: intake gives energy for output. We feed our minds to assimilate and put into action.

That means we read and learn with expectations. But they are based, not on our abilities, but on God: *Happy are they who hope in the Lord!*

Luke 9:22-25 puts that hope to the test.

> If any want to become my followers, let them deny themselves and take up their cross daily and follow me. For those who want to save their life will lose it, and those who lose their life for my sake will save it.

What Jesus gives as the "entrance exam" to discipleship is humanly impossible to accept or do. Peter's first act after receiving the "keys of the Kingdom" was to reject it. He gave the spontaneous reaction of us all.[3]

But Jesus didn't come to teach a human way of life. He calls us to live on the level of God and empowers us to do it. That is why, ultimately, his words and no others teach us to be Christian. We listen to the divine words of the divine Word made flesh in order to give flesh to his words in human actions that are divine. That is Christian discipleship.

[1] *Acts* 2:42.
[2] *John* 1:4; 8:12. See also *Psalm* 27:1; 36:9; 56:13; *Proverbs* 6:23.
[3] *Matthew* 16:21-22.

Initiative: Make the choice. Commit during Lent to learning from Jesus.

MARCH 11, 2011

A broken, humbled heart, O God, you will not scorn (Psalm 51).

Jesus was a disciple. As a boy, and later as a young man, he learned from Scripture and from the rabbis. When he got separated from his parents in Jerusalem, "they found him in the temple, sitting among the teachers, listening... asking them questions."[1]

How did his heart resonate to these words from **Isaiah 58:1-9**?

> This is the fast that I choose: to loose the bonds of injustice...to let the oppressed go free.... to share your bread with the hungry, and bring the homeless poor into your house....

Was he thinking of this when he announced his mission to the people he grew up with in Nazareth:

> The Spirit of the Lord is upon me, because he has anointed me to bring good news to the poor. He has sent me to proclaim release to the captives and recovery of sight to the blind, to let the oppressed go free, to proclaim the year of the Lord's favor.

Jesus came with good news. It was light and life.

> Then your light shall break forth like the dawn, and your healing shall spring up quickly... the glory of the LORD shall be your rear guard. Then you shall call, and the LORD will answer; you shall cry for help, and he will say, "Here I am."

Jesus came with good news. He knew it was good news: *the* Good News. And Lent is a time to hear it. What is it, essentially—in a nutshell?

In **Matthew 9:14-15** Jesus tells us it is *relationship*. The heart and soul of Christianity is relationship—first with Jesus himself, and through him with God as Father and with the Spirit as indwelling Advocate and Guide.

The Pharisees—and those who grew up under their influence—saw religion as *doing*. If you did the right things you were religious. If you didn't, you weren't. And the "right things" were spelled out in the Law. If we look, we may find the same attitude in ourselves.

The disciples of John the Baptizer reflected this assumption when they asked, "Why is it that while we and the Pharisees fast, your disciples do not?" It was taken for granted that if you were "holy," fasting was what you did.

Jesus said no. Nothing makes us "holy" but relationship with God. And he made that the same as relationship with himself. Fasting, he taught, is not just something you do; fasting is to *express* something. What it expresses is the "mourning" of unsatisfied spiritual hunger, longing for himself: "How can the wedding guests go in mourning so long as the groom is with them?" But "When the day comes that the groom is taken away, then they will fast."

Lent invites us to ask what all our actions express, beginning with our religious actions. *Why* do we go to Mass? To "be there" or to *interact* with God? (The reality of relationship is interaction). Interact how? In how many ways? How in the *Introductory Rites*? How during the *Liturgy of the Word*? To answer that is a good start on Lent.

[1]*Luke* 2:46.

Initiative: Be a thinker. Ask what you are expressing when you act.

March 12, 2011

Teach me your way, O Lord, that I may be faithful in your sight (Psalm 86).

Isaiah 58:9-14 presents two levels of response to God, and two levels of promise.

The first level is to keep the Commandments on the "second tablet" of the "two tablets of the covenant," that God gave to Moses on Mount Sinai. Custom assigns to the first tablet the Commandments that call us "to acknowledge God as the one Lord of all and to worship him alone for his infinite holiness." On the second are the Commandments that rule our interaction with humans, "the summary and foundation of which is the commandment of love of neighbor."[1] The Lord promises:

> If you offer your food to the hungry and satisfy the needs of the afflicted [the "second tablet"], then "the Lord will guide you continually, and satisfy your needs.... The ancient ruins shall be rebuilt... you shall be called the repairer of the breach, the restorer of streets to live in." To live by God's law brings well-being on earth, restores and renews human society.

But to those who keep the "first tablet," God promises something higher:

> If you refrain from trampling the sabbath, from pursuing your own interests on my holy day; if you call the sabbath a delight and ... honor it.... then you shall take delight in the LORD, and I will make you ride upon the heights of the earth; I will nourish you with the heritage of your ancestor Jacob....

Treat those on earth right, and we will have delight on earth. Treat God right, and we will "delight in the Lord" himself. We will know God.

Which shall we choose? To focus on living well (in both senses) on earth, or to focus on relationship with God and enjoying that "life to the full" Jesus came to give, finding our delight in knowing God and spending our lives to make his name "hallowed" by every person in the world? This is not an "either-or" choice; we must make it "both-and." *Teach me your way, O Lord, that I may be faithful in your sight.*[2]

Luke 5:27-32 tells us only the hungry will come to be fed. If we are good enough not to think we are bad, we may settle for ordinary, decent human behavior, with no further hunger or desire, no longing to learn how to live on the level of God. This is the curse of the self-controlled; the fallacy of the Pharisees. Jesus calls it the handicap of the "healthy." It is the "good" that is the enemy of the "better."

The paradox is, if we are fully "natural" we will long for the "supernatural." The built-in desire of our intellect and will is for truth and goodness. If the infinite Truth and Goodness we can never attain by nature is offered, it is a sin against our human nature to refuse it.

[1] See *Exodus* 31:18 and John Paul II, *The Splendor of Truth*, nos. 11-13, citing *Exodus* 20:2-11 for the "first tablet" and *Romans* 13:8-10 for the second.
[2] *John* 10:10. See John Paul's brilliant explanation of how Jesus transformed the practice and promise of both tablets in *The Splendor of Truth*, nos. 11 to end.

Initiative: To be fully "natural," long and live for the "supernatural."

TO WHAT DOES LENT CALL US?
QUESTIONS FOR REFLECTION AND DISCUSSION

for the "half week" between Ash Wednesday and the First Sunday of Lent.

Lent is a time for "metanoia," a change of mind. This is *discipleship*: To read, reflect on the word of God, call into question goals, attitudes, priorities, lifestyle.

Invitation:

Take time to think. Ask where you are going spiritually. Join a discussion group. Make changes in your priorities, time-schedule, interests. Check your focus.

Ask yourself in prayer and others in discussion, for each statement below: Do you see this in the Scripture reading? What response does it invite?

Joel 2:12-18: Lent summons us as individuals to convert as a community. Whom does our "community" include?

Matthew 6:1-18: We have to embrace *both* "religion," *and* "spirituality."

The watchword for Christian authenticity is "both-and" as opposed to "either-or."

One's interior, divine act of sharing in God's knowledge, might "take flesh" in human concepts and words that do not perfectly agree with the truth we possess in faith. We "possess" more than we "profess."

2Corinthians 5:20 to 6:2: Is it time to open our doors to everyone we recognize as having "become Christ" through Baptism?

Deuteronomy 30:15-20: The basic "either-or" choice of human existence (post revelation) is to listen to God's words and try to act on them; or to refuse.

We read God's word with expectations based not on our abilities, but on God.

Luke 9:22-25: Jesus did not come to teach a human way of life. He calls us to live on the level of God and empowers us to do it.

Isaiah 58:1-9 and Matthew 9:14-15: The heart and soul of Christianity is *relationship* with Jesus and through him with the Father and Spirit.

The Pharisees see religious acts as *doing*. Jesus sees them as *expressions* of relationship.

Isaiah 58:9-14: Two levels of response to God are: 1. To focus on living well (in both senses) on earth; 2. To focus on relationship with God and "life to the full."

The first focus brings well-being on earth, restores and renews human society. The second brings "delight in the Lord" himself.

Luke 5:27-32: If we are good enough not to feel we are bad, we may settle for decent human behavior. But it is "unnatural" not to long for the "supernatural."

Initiatives:

Participate in both Catholic and Protestant Lenten observances.

Make the choice: commit during Lent to learning from Jesus.

Be a thinker. Ask what you are expressing when you act.

March 13, 2011
Entering Discipleship: the Recognition of Sin

INVENTORY

To what do I attribute the evils in our society? Do I blame them on bad politics? Bad business practices? Inadequate education? Unenlightened ministry in the Church? Disintegrating family life? What do I think is the *root* cause?

Could the root of it all be *sin*?

The *Entrance Antiphon* quotes God: "When they call to me, I will answer them; I will be with them in trouble, I will rescue them and honor them" (*Psalm* 91).

Do I believe the answer to society's problems is to call on God? How often do I do it? And what do I call on him for?

INPUT

In the *Opening Prayer* we ask God to "help us understand the *meaning* of your Son's death and resurrection." But we are not looking just for abstract enlightenment. We continue: "Teach us to reflect it in our lives." We are willing to *respond* to what God shows us, to *act* on what we understand.

The *Prayer over the Gifts* echoes this: "Lord… may this sacrifice help us to *change our lives.*" And so does the *Prayer After Communion*: "Help us to *live by your words* and to *seek Christ*, our bread of life."

The focus of Lent is on *seeing more clearly* and *acting more consistently*. This is the description of *conversion*—but of conversion based on greater insight, on new discovery, on a clearer understanding of what Jesus really calls us to believe and do. We don't just turn away from "the same old sins." We turn away from attitudes, values, priorities, and patterns of behavior we never recognized before as "sin."

This is what "conversion" really means: a "change of mind" made fully human in a change of heart and habits. The New Testament word for sin is *hamartia*, which means "to miss the mark, to fall short." To "convert" is to correct our *aim*: to rectify coordinates and range.

But to do this we have to recognize it when we "miss the mark." We do this in a "*confession* of sin" that is a *profession* of more enlightened faith.

SIN IS THE ROOT:

Genesis 2:7 to 3:7 is a story God told to answer one of the basic questions in life—like the questions little children ask their parents—"Why is there pain and suffering in the world?"

The Genesis story is intended to make it clear that God didn't will this. God does not want people to suffer. The world God gave the first humans to live in was like a garden, teeming with beautiful trees and luscious fruit. A paradise.

But God made humans free. He knew they might abuse their freedom and mess up the world for themselves and others. So he gave instructions: he told them what they must avoid and what they must do if they wanted to keep their living conditions, their environment—including their interaction with one another—pleasant, beautiful, and enjoyable for all. These instructions have come down to us as the "Ten Commandments."

In the story there is only one command, because the point of the story is that there is only one cause of all the pain and suffering in the world. The cause is *sin*—the choice people make to use freedom, not to obey God, but to disregard God's instructions and do what they themselves think will make them happy. We might think some particular sin is messing up the world, some particular way of acting. But God says the problem is sin as such. Any time we choose not to do what God says, we "miss the mark" and we mess up the world for ourselves and others.

When we choose to live by our own light, our own guidance system, instead of God's, the results are disastrous. When we recognize this, our "eyes are opened" and we realize we are blind. Then there is hope.

"IF YOU ARE..."

Matthew 4:1-11 shows us Jesus confronting his call to be the Messiah, the Savior of the world. He is being tempted to falsify his mission. Not to disobey God overtly and explicitly, but to adopt as the goal of his mission something that looks good to human eyes but "misses the mark" established by God's wisdom. "If you are the Son of God, give bread."

The devil urges him to give people what they think they want: prosperity, protection from enemies, a just and peaceful society; in other words, a pleasant, pain-free life on this earth. Basically, the devil is urging Jesus to make the earth a garden without God.

Jesus is not asked to exclude God; just to make God marginal. God can be a player; just don't let God call all the plays. God will be allowed to speak to those who want to listen, but listening to God is not what will save the world. Society believes salvation consists in what people have, not in what they hear.

Jesus' first answer is a call to *discipleship*—to listening and learning. The way to live fully is to live "by every word that comes from the mouth of God." Is this an answer I have accepted? Will I accept to be the one who saves society around me by preparing myself through reading and reflecting on the words of God? Is my failure to do this the place where I am "missing the mark"? Can I recognize this as "sin"?

"THROUGH ONE MAN"

The *Responsorial Psalm* is a meditation on the first reading. The response to which it guides us is: *"Be merciful, Lord, for we have sinned."* When we realize we are blind, we call out to God. And God will always save us. The "definition of God" that God himself gave when he showed his "glory" to Moses is: "a God merciful and gracious, slow to anger, and abounding in steadfast love and faithfulness" (*Exodus* 34:6). God will never turn away from us when we sin. But for us to turn to God we have to *recognize* our sin: Jesus said to the Pharisees, who refused to do this, "Because you say, 'We see,' your sin remains" (read *John*, chapter 9).

Romans 5:12-19 shows us the form God's mercy took when he acted to save us from our sins. And it gives the answer we asked for in the *Opening Prayer:* "Father, help us understand the *meaning* of your Son's death and resurrection."

On the cross Jesus recognized sin as sin in the name of us all. He "became sin" by taking our sins into his own body (*2Corinthians* 5:21) to express and expiate the evil of sin in the name of the whole human race. And just as sin and suffering entered the world through one free choice—the first human choice to sin—so salvation began through the free choice of "one man," Jesus Christ, to offer himself on the cross. When he died, all who were or ever would be made members of his body by acceptance of him also died "in him," and their sins were annihilated. This is the mystery of our redemption.

But just as the first human act of disobedience to God began a chain reaction that filled the world with sin, so Jesus' unique divine-human act of obedience began a chain reaction of graced responses to God that continues to reverse the destructive effects of sin on human society. Through the obedience of "one man," we were saved. But through the obedience of many, that salvation takes flesh in society to turn wasteland into gardens, alienation into acceptance, selfishness into service, and indifference into love. For this to happen, however, each one of us has to be that "one man" or "one woman" in whom it begins.

This may be the conversion to which God calls us during Lent.

INSIGHT:

Do I really believe that if I want to relieve pain and suffering in the world, the first thing I should do is read and reflect—seriously and consistently—on the words of God? Should this be my first priority?

INITIATIVE:

What "conversion" will I work toward during Lent? What would it mean for me to convert to being a disciple? How could I begin?

MARCH 14, 2011

The *Responsorial* (*John* 6:63 and *Psalm* 19) could be the motto for the discipleship to which the *Liturgy of the Word* calls us in every Mass: "*Your words, Lord, are spirit and life.*"

Leviticus 19:1-18 puts morality in context: "Be holy, for I, your God, am holy." Christian morality is not "being good," it is "being like." And its goal is *relationship*: with God and others. Once the "grace of the Lord Jesus Christ" was revealed as "the favor of sharing in God's own life," the goal of a moral life became mystical *union*: union with God in one shared life; union with others in the "communion of the Holy Spirit."

"You shall not steal... lie... swear falsely...." We can just accept and obey, or we can *ask*, like *disciples*, "Why? Why are these words 'spirit and life'?"

The answer is, sins destroy *relationship*. Stealing says property is more important than people. Lying makes words mean nothing and communication impossible. To "profane the name of God" means we don't care to know or relate to God as God really is. Those who have the slightest real knowledge of God cry out, "Hallowed be your Name!"

Look to the *goal* of every law, even God's. God doesn't want us just to obey; he wants us to be one with him in mind and heart. This makes the difference between Phariseeism and friendship with God; between mere "followers" and "disciples." The *Re-sponsorial Psalm* pilots us: "*The law of the Lord is perfect... giving wisdom to the simple.*"

"You shall not defraud, curse, mislead, slander, or fail to help your neighbor." The Commandments of the "second tablet" have as their base and goal, "You shall love your neighbor as yourself." But the Psalm roots this in "fear of the Lord," which, divorced from fright, is *perspective*. If there were no God, people might vie for dominance, some claiming to be greater than others and entitled to more. But if our very existence is an ongoing act and gift of God, we are all equally nothing before him. And equally precious. All are "as ourselves." "*The command of the Lord is clear, enlightening the eye.*" God's laws give perspective.

"You shall not bear hatred, take revenge, or hold a grudge." Love endures evil in others. Because God does. The Jewish Scriptures repeat forty-three times, "His *steadfast love* endures forever." And John's Gospel introduces Jesus as "enduring love." If we keep God and his love in perspective, our love for others will not be fragmented or fail: "*The fear of the Lord is pure, enduring forever.*"[1]

Matthew 25:31-46: Our relationship with God will be judged by our relationship with others: "If you did it for one of mine, you did it for me." And vice-versa. To love others "as ourselves" is to love them as Christ, because by Baptism we "became Christ." Now our perspective is mystery.

[1]*John* 1:17; 1970 *New American Bible*; *Luke* 6:35-36; *1Corinthians* 13:4-8.

Initiative: Be a disciple: ask "Why?" about every word of God's law. Study God.

March 15, 2011

The *Responsorial* (*Psalm* 34) assures us: *"From all their afflictions, God will deliver the just."*

Isaiah 55:10-11 tells us how he does it: God saves us through his "word": "It will not return to me void, but shall... achieve the end for which I sent it."

This is not just God's creative word. He compares it to the "rain and snow" that "water the earth, making it fertile and fruitful." That is what God's word does for us. It makes us fertile in life-giving ideas and fruitful in the lives we lead and help others to lead. We need to take in God's word the way we take in food and water. If we do, *"From all their afflictions, God will deliver the just."*

The *Responsorial Psalm* emphasizes two kinds of prayer that "deliver" us. The first is the prayer that the *Liturgy of the Word* encourages in us: meditation, "faith seeking understanding" through reflection: "I *sought* the Lord, and he answered me and delivered me from all my fears." Jesus said, "Seek and you will find; knock, and the door will be opened for you." He also said, "If you remain in my word, [immersed in it, absorbed in trying to learn and live it] you will truly be my *disciples* and you will know the truth, and the truth will set you free." Free from destructive errors and distortions; free from fears and anxieties. Prayer helps us see God and the world in perspective. In that view, God reigns supreme and there is no room for fear. *"From all their afflictions, God will deliver the just."*[1]

Matthew 6:7-15 teaches us a second way to pray: the way Jesus taught his disciples:[2] The "Our Father" is "petitionary prayer," but it is also instructive. It makes a list of Jesus' own priorities and tells us to adopt them as our own. If we pray for these petitions above all others, thinking about what we are saying, we will grow into union with the mind and heart of Christ. This is also a prayer of discipleship.

Every petition in the *Our Father* is asking for Christ's triumph, which will be complete at the end of the world.[3] What is delaying it? If God's word "will not return void, but shall achieve the end for which he sent it," why is the Kingdom not yet established?

The answer is simple: there are not enough disciples on earth who are truly immersed in his word—enough to understand and live it. We tend to settle for keeping the laws, without learning where they come from or where they intend to lead us. Even some teachers in the Church just learn doctrines and laws, without seeking deep understanding of the mind and heart of God from whence they came, and pass shallow understanding on to others. Jesus calls them the blind leading the blind. There is no substitute for deep, personal discipleship.[4]

[1]*Psalm* 34:4; *Matthew* 7:7; *John* 8:31-32.
[2]*Luke* 11:1.
[3]See "The Pater Noster As An Eschatological Prayer" in Raymond E. Brown, S.S., *New Testament Essays*, Bruce, 1965; Doubleday, Image Books, 1968.
[4]See *Matthew* 15:12-14.

Initiative: Be a disciple. Ask where every law comes from and where it leads.

MARCH 16, 2011

The *Responsorial* (*Psalm* 51) is an insight into God: *"A broken, humbled heart, O God, you will not scorn."*

Jonah 3:1-10 is a story of conversion. That is what Lent is all about and what the *Liturgy of the Word* calls us to: *metanoia*. We translate the word as "repentance," but it literally means more: a "change of mind," a "complete makeover" of all that determines who we are as persons: our life-goal; means chosen to achieve it; priority given to those means over the means to lesser or even contradictory goals. *Metanoia* is direction-finding. And what initiates and sustains it is response to God's voice, however it is received.

Continued attention to God's voice, and continued response to it, is called *discipleship*. Lent is offered as a short time of intense discipleship to give an extra push to *metanoia*.

The people of Nineveh got the invitation, responded, and were saved. The Scripture says, "God repented of the evil he had threatened to do to them." What Scripture calls God's "repentance" is just the mirror-image we see of our own—just as the "evil" God threatens is in reality God's observation of the evil we are already doing to ourselves.

Is there any difference between Jonah's voice sounding in the streets of Nineveh—"Forty days more and Nineveh shall be destroyed"—and God's voice sounding in our ears through the readings proclaimed in the *Liturgy of the Word*? The Church says there isn't.

What we say appears in the action we take or don't take in response.

Forty days? Forty years? The timeframe is not the message. The message is, "Sin is destroying us; conversion will save us." The carrot and the stick; if we doubt either one we are fools. But the carrot is the one to focus on. "Repentance" is a joyful word in Scripture, because the call to it always includes the promise of the Holy Spirit poured out to "create a clean heart" in us and "renew within us a steadfast spirit." "Repent" is really a proclamation about God: *"A broken, humbled heart, O God, you will not scorn."*

In **Luke 11:29-32** Jesus says, "You have a greater than Jonah here." Is he still saying that? To us? If so, where is he? Can we hear his voice?

The "sign of Jonah" is the Church. Jesus risen from the dead was a "sign" to those who saw him. But he is only a sign today when he is visible, and visibly risen from the dead in the Church that is his body. In us.

When we "rise" from the death and darkness of whatever pit our culture led us into, we are the "sign of Jonah." When we live in a way that reveals the divine life of Christ in us, we are the sign of Jonah. To those who "sit in darkness and the shadow of death" Jesus warned, "no other sign will be given."

That puts a heavy responsibility on us. But if we let Jesus carry it *with*, *in*, and *through* us, we will find the shared yoke easy and the shared burden light.

Initiative: Be a sign. Live a lifestyle inexplicable without the life of God in you.

March 17, 2011

The *Responsorial* (*Psalm* 138) is a testimony *"O Lord, on the day I called for help you answered me!"*

Esther chapter C (after chapter 4), **verses 12, 14-16, 23-25** shows us what it means to live a lifestyle inexplicable to those who do not recognize the empowering presence of grace—the divine life of God—in us.

Esther laid it out before God: "I am alone and have no help but you." Do you know people who are alone? Who really have no one to help them but God? Don't you worry about them?

Sure: logically, saying this is like facing a mugger and saying, "I have no one to help me but a whole division of United States Marines." If we have God, what else do we need? But that isn't the way we see it when God is all we have.

It isn't the way others see it either. To attempt something—anything—with no help available but God's seems crazy. His help is good in theory, but in practice we don't like to depend on it. So if we do attempt the impossible when we are "alone and have no help but God," that bears witness to God's life in us—even before we succeed.

Let's don't think in terms of business ventures and other unimportant projects whose outcome won't make any difference to you a hundred years from now. Let's talk about essentials. A temptation you are fighting that all your friends keep convoying you into. Ideals you hold that no one under-

stands or agrees with; that you are not even sure you believe in. Values Jesus taught that just don't seem to make sense to you. Times when neither your feelings nor your mind are much help to you in doing what nevertheless you know God wants you to do. Then can you join Esther in telling God, "I am alone and have no help but you"?

What if you are blocked from Confession because of something you "know you can't stop?" What if the last priest you talked to was harsh and discouraging? What does it reveal about your faith if you keep trying? You may find yourself saying, *"O Lord, on the day I called for help you answered me!"*

As long as we have God's promises we are not alone; they are comforting company. So are the stories of the way God "fulfilled his promises" to others. They are there in the Bible. Read them. The *Liturgy of the Word* invites us to do a little discipleship. Read how Esther's story turned out.

In **Matthew 7:7-12** Jesus makes some promises. "Ask... Seek... Knock.... The one who asks receives, who seeks finds, who knocks enters." Ask when you don't know how it can be given to you. Seek when you don't know how you can possibly find it. Keep knocking on a stone wall. The divine life of God in you reveals itself through faith in the midst of doubt, "hope that contradicts hope," and "love that surpasses knowledge." That makes you the "sign of Jonah."[1]

[1]See *Romans* 4:18; *Ephesians* 3:19.

Initiative: Read Scripture. Learn how God helps those who trust him.

MARCH 18, 2011

The *Responsorial* (*Psalm* 130) is both truth and trust: *"If you, O Lord, laid bare our guilt, who could endure it?"*

Ezekiel 18:21-28 basically tells us that God doesn't keep books.

Many of us grew up thinking God keeps all our sins recorded in a big ledger, along with all the good things we do to make up for them. At the "judgment," when we die, God subtracts one from the other and we have to make up the difference in "Purgatory." We took for granted the good list would be shorter.

But Ezekiel talks as if the only thing that counts is what side you are on at the end: "If the wicked turns away from all the sins he has committed... he shall surely live, he shall not die. None of the crimes he has committed shall be remembered against him." And vice-versa: "If the virtuous man turns from the path of virtue to do evil.... none of his good deeds shall be remembered." So how do you run up a score?

God doesn't keep score. What matters to him is not what we have done but what we are. It is true, we "create ourselves" by what we do. Every act, good or bad, changes us, for better or worse. But the change isn't quantitative; it is cumulative. What counts is the part all of our actions play in making it easier or harder for us to surrender ourselves totally to God in death. In pure faith, hope, and love. The last judgment we make about God is our personal Last Judgment. Either we want him enough to say "Yes" to death—and to leaving all we have and love on earth, including life itself, to possess him—or we don't. Our answer at that moment is all that counts.

Matthew 5:20-26 seems both to support this and contradict it. Jesus bases God's judgment on the kind of person we are: loving or unloving. All the examples speak of this: embraced anger, abusive language, silent contempt, alienation; they say we are or are not living in love. It's a pass-fail exam. No one adds or subtracts points.

But if we haven't completely reconciled our differences with others, Jesus uses the image of a prison from which we "will not be released until you have paid the last penny." This seems quantitative.

Does Jesus speak of "punishment"? No. "Paid the last penny" can as easily mean "made a complete turnaround," or "grown to the fullness of love." The image speaks of completeness, not of payment as such.

But if we think of "penalty" instead of "punishment," that works. God doesn't "punish" us for sins; what would be the point of it? But he warns us that if we do not try to grow into "the perfection of love," there will be distance to make up before we enter heaven. To say "Yes" to death, choosing God as our All with love undivided between God and any creature, is not something that comes easily. If we don't work at growing into this (which means surrendering to it) during life, then the natural consequence or "penalty" is that we might have a struggle at the end. Another reason to embrace discipleship.

Initiative: Seek the "perfection of love." Use the *Liturgy of the Word*.

March 19, 2011

St. Joseph, Husband of Mary, Foster Father of Jesus

The readings for the feast of St. Joseph are all about faith, hope, and promise.

In **Matthew 1:16-24** the angel tells Joseph "do not be afraid to take Mary as your wife." What was he afraid of? We usually assume that Joseph thought Mary, to whom he was engaged, was pregnant by another man, and for that reason was going to break off the engagement and "dismiss her quietly."

Another interpretation is that Mary told Joseph exactly what had happened, and he believed her. He was intending to take Mary as the wife who would be the mother of his children. But when Yahweh, the LORD, made it known that he had chosen his fiancée to be the mother of his own Son, Joseph's reaction, as a devout Jew, was to back off in reverent "fear of the Lord."

The angel affirmed that Joseph was to be Mary's husband anyway—and fulfill the role of earthly father to Jesus. "You are to name him," the angel said, which was the father's prerogative. But the real Father, Yahweh, chose the name: "You are to name him Jesus...."

Thus Joseph had a double role: as the one everybody assumed to be Jesus' real father,[1] he was to be for Jesus everything a father should be on earth. But he was to exercise his role as "steward" of God the Father, whose place he held. And see his son Jesus always through eyes of faith that told him whose Son Jesus really was.

Christian mothers and fathers must see their children as more God's than theirs. At Baptism, parents deliver their children over to death. Yes. Shocking, but true. We are incorporated into the body of Jesus on the cross to die in him and rise with him to live for nothing except to let Jesus continue his divine mission in our body, through our human words and actions. Christian parents are charged to raise their children as divine, to live on the level of God. Could that cause doubt and fear?

We need *faith* to see our own children as divine: bodies in whom Jesus Christ is living and acting. **2Samuel 7:4-16** calls us to add *hope* to that. Nathan tells David, God "will raise up your offspring after you... and I will establish the throne of his kingdom forever."

In spite of David's sins, God kept his promise to him—and will keep the promise he made implicitly to us when he called us to be parents: that if we remain conscious in faith and steadfast in hope, "blessed is the fruit of your womb.... I appointed you to go and bear fruit, fruit that will last."[2]

We don't always see God's grace reigning in our children. **Romans 4:13-22** shows us Abraham "hoping against hope" when it seemed his son, Isaac, was lost to him forever. Hope is based, not on what we see, but on what we hear. We find it in God's word. "*The Son of David will live forever*" (*Responsorial, Psalm* 89). Whose child do we have?

[1] *Matthew* 13:33; *Luke* 3:23; 4:22.
[2] *Luke* 1:42; *John* 15:16.

Initiative: Believe in what is. Hope in what can be. Work for it with love.

(SAME DAY)

The *Responsorial* (*Psalm* 119) asserts the blessing of discipleship: *"Happy are they who follow the law of the Lord."*

Deuteronomy 26:16-19: A principle of American jurisprudence is: "Ignorance of the law is no excuse." For Christians, to seek knowledge of God's law is a commitment.

Moses told the People, "Today you are making this agreement with the Lord: he is to be your God and you are to walk in his ways," observing all of God's "statutes, commandments, and decrees."

Obviously, we can't live by all of God's principles and ideals if we don't know what they are. And there is too much to learn overnight. Or over a lifetime. If it were just a matter of "statutes, commandments, and decrees," we could learn them in one catechism course! But the point of the Covenant is to absorb God's mind and heart so completely through reflection on his words and wonders that we will "love the Lord our God with all our heart, soul and mind." For this the *Liturgy of the Word* invites us to become *disciples*.

There is more. The People are agreeing to live in a way that shows them to be "a people peculiarly his own." "Peculiarly" just means "especially," but the word makes a point: Any group of people who live by the ideals and principles God teaches will, in fact, seem "peculiar" to the unenlightened. Jesus calls his disciples to a radical peculiarity.

In **Matthew 5:43-48** Jesus zooms in on the "scandalous commandment," the one that drew instant protest out of Peter.[1] "Love your enemies, pray for your persecutors." This just isn't human. Every soldier we put in the field and every bomb we drop declares we would all as a nation rather kill our enemies than be killed loving them.

There is no escaping Jesus' meaning. He declares categorically, "If any want to become my followers, let them... take up their cross and follow me. Those who want to save their life will lose it. Those who lose their life for my sake will find it." But we prefer to save our lives by killing our enemies (perhaps sending them to Hell, since they are presumably the "bad guys") rather than let them send us to heaven by giving up our lives in love as Jesus did on the cross. According to Jesus, this is what God finds "peculiar."

This is exactly what makes Jesus' point when he says, "This will prove you are children of your heavenly Father...." Anybody who loves, not as humans do, but as God alone does, must be doing so by sharing in God's divine life. It is above all by observing this commandment, treating every man and woman on earth as our brother or sister, that we reveal ourselves as the mystery of Christ's risen body on earth, children of God the Father.

Obviously, it takes a lot of discipleship to grow into this one.

[1]See *Matthew* 16:21-28. The basic principle here is that we love others, even enemies, enough to let them kill us rather than do them harm. This is just as shocking to us as it was to the first disciples.

Initiative: Don't give up. To love like God is a graduate course. Keep at it.

FOR REFLECTION AND DISCUSSION: LENT WEEK ONE

The answer to sin is to see—and act. *Discipleship* is the alternative to darkness. If we are committed *students* of the mind and heart of God, his truth will free us.

Invitation: Get something really great out of Lent this year. If you decide to go for it, these daily reflections will "call the plays" for you. All you have to do is run them.

Ask yourself in prayer and others in discussion, for each statement below: Do you see this in the Scripture reading? What response does it invite?

Sunday: There is only one cause of all the pain and suffering in the world. The cause is *sin*.

Society believes happiness comes from what people have, not from what they hear. Jesus' first "saving act" is a call to *discipleship*—to listening and learning.

Monday: Christian morality is not "being good," it is "being like." Its goal is *relationship*: with God and others.

Look to the *goal* of every law, even God's. God doesn't want us just to obey; he wants us to be one with him in mind and heart.

To love others "as ourselves" is to love them as Christ does, because by Baptism we "became Christ." This makes our perspective mystery.

Tuesday: God saves us initially through his "word." It makes us fertile in life-giving ideas and fruitful in the lives we lead.

Wednesday: "Repentance" is a joyful word in Scripture, because the call to it always includes the promise of the Holy Spirit.

The "sign of Jonah" is the Church living in a way that reveals the divine life of Christ in us.

Thursday: The divine life of God in us reveals itself through faith in the midst of doubt, "hope that contradicts hope," and "love that surpasses knowledge." Explain.

Friday: What matters to God is not what we have done but what we are.

Saturday: We are committed by the Covenant to work at absorbing God's mind and heart so completely through reflection on his words and wonders that we will "love the Lord our God with all our heart, soul, and mind." For this the *Liturgy of the Word* invites us to become *disciples*.

Decisions:

Be a disciple. Ask where every law comes from and where it leads.
Be a sign. Learn from Scripture how to live a lifestyle inexplicable without the life of God in you.

MARCH 20, 2011
The Event and the Glory that Motivate Discipleship

INVENTORY

How much do I think about the *event* of Christ's death and resurrection? Do I consciously base my whole life on the difference that event has made?

The *Entrance Antiphon* asks: "Remember your mercies, Lord, your tenderness from ages past." Do I use my *memory* of God's deeds in a way that gives me confidence God "will not let our enemies triumph over us"? Do I let the *Liturgy of the Word* remind me of what God has done in the past?

INPUT

In the *Opening Prayer* we are looking for understanding, and for the *vision of a goal* that will encourage us: "*Enlighten* us with your word, that we may find the way to your glory."

Jesus is the Word made flesh. His words are "spirit and life." In the *Liturgy of the Word* we hear his voice, as we hear that of the Father. The Church teaches: "In the sacred books the Father who is in heaven *meets his children* with great love and *speaks with them.* And the force and power in the word of God is so great that it remains the support and energy of the Church." But to receive that power and support we have to *listen* to God's words. And so we ask God, "Help us to hear your Son." [1]

God's answer will be to *show us Jesus,* to let us see his glory so that when we lose sight of it we will *remember,* continue to listen to his words and follow his way.

[1] *John* 6:63; *Vatican II,* "Liturgy," no. 33.

GOD'S INTERVENTION:

The *Responsorial (Psalm 33)* asks, "*Lord, let your mercy be on us, as we place our trust in you.*" To "have mercy" is to come to the aid of another out of a sense of *relationship.* And relationship is the result of *interaction.* It is on the basis of God's interaction with us that we say "*We place our trust in you.*"

Genesis 12:1-4 tells us that it all began with the *event* of God's intervening in history to form a special relationship with one man—Abraham—and his descendants. This relationship was a covenant that committed God to take an active, guiding role in human history.[1] "Go from your country and your kindred and your father's house to the land that I will show you. I will make of you a great nation, and I will bless you, and make your name great."

This is the act of *mercy*—of God's entering into a special relationship with Abraham's race—that is the first foundation of our trust. God's promise to Abraham was realized in Jesus, in whom all those who become members of his body, the Church, are "sons and daughters in the Son," children of God and children of Abraham. In Christ the promise is fulfilled: "All the communities of the earth shall find blessing in you."

REVEALED IN JESUS:

2Timothy 1:8-10 tells us that the full favor (grace) of the plan God began to implement through Abraham was "made manifest through the appearance of our Savior," Jesus Christ. Through the Good News of his life, death, and resurrection Jesus "has brought life and immortality into clear light." And he "has called us to a holy life."

We know through the Gospel that this "holy life" is actually divine life. Through Baptism we were incorporated into the body of Jesus on the cross, into the *event* of his dying and rising. We died to our merely natural, human lives and rose to live as sharers in the divine life of Jesus. Our glory is to "be Christ." And his glory is to be visibly, manifestly alive and risen in us. St. Irenaeus wrote: "Life in humans is the glory of God." Christ's glory, the proof of his resurrection and triumph, is his divine life present and shining out unmistakably in those he has redeemed.

To live authentically as Christians we need to have some idea of the glory Jesus has in himself, and of how that glory should appear in us who are his body on earth. To understand what that glory is and should be, the *Liturgy of the Word* invites us to reflect deeply on the Scriptures. That is why we prayed in the *Opening Prayer*, "Enlighten us with your *word*, that we may find the *way* to your glory."

A VISION OF HIS GLORY:

In **Matthew 17:1-9** Jesus took three of his disciples—the same three he would take with him later in his agony in the garden—and led them up to the top of a mountain, where he was "transfigured before their eyes." Something of the glory he had as God appeared visibly in his body—but only a very little bit, because they were still able to speak.

When Peter suggested, however, that they should put Jesus on a par with Moses and Elijah, who embodied the Law and the Prophets, by building shrines to the three of them, the Father made it clear that Jesus was not on a par with anyone: he was infinitely superior to every human prophet or saint, no matter how great. *"This,"* the Father declared, "is *my beloved Son."* And he spoke from within the *shekinah*, a cloud both opaque and luminous, which in Scripture is a sign of God's presence. The Father added: *"Listen* to him!"

We keep getting the same message. If we really want confidence that God "will not let our enemies triumph over us," we need to *listen* to his Son. If we want a motivating goal for our life, we need to take seriously Christ's glory and ours, and keep striving to enter into it through deeper understanding and love.

We do this by reflecting on the words of God that show us his glory revealed in the Word made flesh. Jesus is not just an exemplary human being; he is God himself showing us how God would and did live in human flesh.

Long ago God spoke to our ancestors in many and various ways by the prophets. But in these last days he has spoken to us by a Son... through whom he also created the worlds.

He is the reflection of God's glory and the exact imprint of God's very being....

And the Word became flesh and lived among us, and we have seen his glory, the glory as of a father's only son, full of grace and truth.

The glory revealed in Jesus is the glory God wants to reveal in us as his divine-human body on earth.

In the Transfiguration, God gave us a glimpse of Jesus in his divine glory so that we would be encouraged to interact with him in his humanity: learning from his words and example how to live as humans who are divine; how to live on the level of God. We learn this by *interacting* with Jesus as *disciples*: reading his words, asking questions, talking to him. But it has to be "hands on" learning. We don't know what Jesus is talking about until we try to actually do what he says. We don't know we are hearing his voice until we respond to his inspirations. We don't experience ourselves as his body until we begin working with him for the establishment of God's reign on earth, asking him to act with us, in us, and through us in everything we do.

The starting point, however, and key to doing this well, is *listening to him*. We first have to become *disciples*, students dedicated to learning from him. For this we pray: "Lord, help us to *hear* your Son."

[1]God's covenant with Noah (*Genesis* 9:9) was only a pledge not to destroy the human race. All who survived the flood are Noah's descendants. But Abram and his family were a particular clan, the descendants of Noah's son Shem (*Genesis* 10:1; 11: 10, 26).

INSIGHT:

By what standard do I measure my behavior? By human standards or God's? By "right or wrong" (i.e. "reasonable") or by "faith-inspired"? By what I see others around me doing, or by what I hear Jesus saying we should do?

INITIATIVE:

Spend some time thinking about Jesus' glory. How do you—or will you—share in it?

MARCH 21, 2011

The *Responsorial* (*Psalm* 79) gives a key to the readings: *"Lord, do not deal with us as our sins deserve."*

In the Gospel Jesus is going to tell us, "Be compassionate, as your Father is compassionate." The reading from **Daniel 9:4-10**: reminds us how much we ourselves need the compassion Jesus instructs us to give to others.

The Book of Daniel is an example of "apocalyptic" writing, which looks ahead to the "day of the Lord" and to the consummation of history when God, the Lord of history, will ultimately vindicate his people. It was written during a bitter persecution, and its purpose was to strengthen and comfort the Jewish people in their ordeal.[1]

Daniel recognizes that troubles always have causes. Frequently they are brought on by our failures to live by the principles God teaches. Historians say the seeds of World War II were planted in the harsh terms of the peace treaty that ended World War I. The scourge of Islamic terrorism today would not be possible if Muslims had no grounds for perceiving America as the society of the Great Satan because of the values we project. These are not our deepest and truest values, but to the superficial scanner, our media present us as a country of materialism, militarism, violence, and sexual license. Our reaction is defensive: we pour billions into national security. Daniel's reaction was to confess his People's sins to God:

Ah, Lord... we have sinned and done wrong… acted wickedly and rebelled, turning aside from your commandments.... We have not listened to your servants, who spoke in your name.

His real message, however, is not about us. It is about God: "Yours, O Lord, are compassion and forgiveness." Every "confession" of sin is a "profession" of faith in God's values and love.

In **Luke 6:36-38** Jesus tells us to set all our standards by the standards God follows. "Be compassionate, as your Father is compassionate." Then he seems to reverse himself and say that God will match his standards to ours: "for the measure you give will be the measure you get back."

The truth is, God never limits his goodness to correspond to ours. When we pray, "Forgive us... as we forgive..." "as" does not mean "in the measure that," but closer to "while." We are anticipating the "wedding banquet of the Lamb," when total reconciliation will reign between all people and with God.

What limits God is our refusal to open ourselves to his generosity. If we close our minds, God cannot enlighten us as he wants. If we close our hearts, God cannot love through us as he wills. If we refuse to forgive, God cannot give us his peace. But never, *never* does God refuse to forgive when we repent, to give when we ask, or to fill us when we admit our emptiness. We already know God's answer when we pray, *"Lord, do not deal with us as our sins deserve."*

[1] Taken from the introduction to the Book of Daniel in the *Catholic Study Bible*, Oxford University, 1990, using the *New American Bible* texts.

Initiative: Listen to the readings. Measure yourself by what you hear.

MARCH 22, 2011

The *Responsorial* (*Psalm* 50) promises: *"To the upright I will show the saving power of God."* Isaiah encourages us to add: "And also to those not upright."

Isaiah 1:10-20 offers forgiveness and purification to the "princes of Sodom." When we read in *Genesis* 19 the sin of Sodom, we wonder at this promise. Lot turned over his own daughters to rapists because in his culture protecting guests was sacrosanct. It was a choice between his guests or his daughters. But even to these rapists God says, "Though your sins be like scarlet, they may become white as snow…. If you are willing and obey, you shall eat the good things of the land." Let's be honest. Would we say that to a child abuser?

To priests guilty of that sin, the Church offers forgiveness; but with no possibility of ever being admitted to full priestly ministry again. That is because we learned—late, after 1980—that no matter how much therapy is given, recidivism can never be discounted. This alerted us to another aspect of sin: one obvious but overlooked.

Bishop Geoffrey Robinson, after nine years on the Australian child-abuse commission, gives this overlooked aspect of sin as a possible reason why so many bishops re-assigned offenders after they repented. We were so focused on seeing sin, including child abuse, as a "direct offense against God," that the bishops treated it as any other sexual sin: confession and absolution marked "end of story." But sin always also does *damage to people.* If we forget this, we might act as if forgiveness precludes forestalling. With our eyes only on repentance we can be blind to risk. The truth is, to forgive fully does not entail the folly of gambling on reform. If we do, it is the psychological and spiritual well-being of children that we wager. No matter what the odds, that is too much to gamble.[1]

In **Matthew 23:1-12** Jesus tells us why we include the *Liturgy of the Word* in every Mass. It is to make sure we have direct exposure to the word of God.

We can never rely entirely on second-hand exposure through teachers, priests, and bishops. In his time Jesus said, "The scribes and Pharisees have succeeded Moses as teachers." That is a possibility in every time. We need to obey every legitimate authority, but as disciples, not dumbbells. We should view all opinions and optional customs in the light of the word of God, expecting some errors.[2]

Jesus mentions some: blind applications of the law that lay "heavy burdens" on people; ways of dressing that suggest some are "higher" than others; preferential treatment and signs of special respect in gatherings; honorific titles. He alone is the teacher; the rest of us, clergy and laity alike, are all fellow-students who must verify by his words what other pupils say they have heard. No one is "higher" than another. Those who want status should seek it through serving others. That is the word of God.

[1] *Confronting Power and Sex in the Catholic Church*, Liturgical Press, 2008, p. 203.
[2] See Vatican II: *Church*, nos. 48, 51; *Church in the Modern World*, no. 19; *Revelation*, no. 8.

Initiative: Assume some errors in ordinary teaching and practice. Try to fix them.

MARCH 23, 2011

The *Responsorial* (*Psalm* 31) prays with confidence: "*Save me, O Lord, in your steadfast love!*"

Jeremiah 18:18-20 affirms a truth of human life as shocking as it is sad. Truth arouses criticism. Good incites to evil. "Must good be repaid with evil, that they would dig a pit for my life?" You can't love people enough to stop them from hating you. Jeremiah couldn't. "Remember that I stood before you to speak in their behalf." Jesus couldn't. And no one who works for renewal in the Church can. Accept it.

But we can count on God: "*Save me, O Lord, in your steadfast love!*"

In **Matthew 20:17-28** Jesus leads us onto dangerous ground. We are Catholics. We have great respect for official religion teachers and for priests. We do, we should, and we must. But Jesus pointed out that his greatest enemies were the "chief priests and scribes." Add the strictest observers of the Law, the Pharisees. These are the three groups we would most expect to welcome him. Instead, they sought to "condemn him to death."

Not once do the Gospels mention the "chief priests" as being in favor of Jesus. They are named as the enemy 54 times. The "elders," which is the correct word for those we call "priests" (from "presbyter") today, are mentioned 24 times as enemies and once as envoys of a rich benefactor. An individual scribe or Pharisee might be good, like Nicodemus, but as a group, out of 54 reports

of interaction with Jesus, they are the enemy all but once, when Luke reports that "some of the scribes answered, 'Teacher, you have spoken well.'" Should this make us anticlerical?

No. It should make us shun *power* for ourselves and mistrust it in others. We should be on guard against all those in positions of authority who, like "those in authority among the Gentiles," want to "lord it" over people and "make their importance felt." They exist. Given human nature and the pretentious protocols we impose on those with power, now taken for granted in the Church, it is a wonder there aren't more.

Jesus was radical about shunning prestige and power. And insistent. "Anyone among you who aspires to greatness must serve the rest. Whoever wants to rank first among you must serve the needs of all."

To help them remember this, the popes have taken the title *servus servorum Dei*: "servant of the servants of God." But we made it hard for them to remember it by insisting on crowning them with a triple crown (which Paul VI stopped wearing and sold) and carrying them through the streets in a sedan chair (which John Paul II discontinued). People still call the pope "Your holiness," and bow or kneel before him. But change is in the air. And the air is the Spirit of God. Every identified abuse is the first blossom of reform. Whatever we see wrong, our response, enlightened by the word of God, will always be, "*Save me, O Lord, in your steadfast love!*"

Initiative: Never read the Scriptures without active faith, hope, and love.

THURSDAY SECOND WEEK IN LENT

MARCH 24, 2011

The *Responsorial* (*Psalm* 1) takes note: *"Happy are they who hope in the Lord."*

If we keep assembling with the community for Mass, the *Liturgy of the Word* assures us that the truth will catch up with us, whether or not we want to hear it. All truth is lifegiving, but sometimes it takes faith to accept that. And all truth offers hope, even if at first it discourages us. Yesterday's reading could have been hard for some priests to hear, especially if they are infected with "clericalism" or "triumphalism." Today's reading might make some of the affluent uncomfortable. But truth is truth, and all truth is lifegiving. And all truth holds out hope. (If it doesn't it is not from God and therefore not truth). If we want to grow through love to the fullness of life, truth is our ally.

Jeremiah 17:5-10 is litmus paper for true and false trust. "Cursed is the one who trusts in human beings," he says. Or in anything created. "Blessed is the one who trusts in the Lord." Everybody trusts in something. Jeremiah tells us to be sure we know what we trust in.

That may not be easy. Jeremiah continues, "More tortuous than all else is the human heart... who can understand it?" The answer is: "God can." "I, the Lord, alone probe the mind and test the heart." And he helps us to know who we are. He does it, first of all, through his word.

It isn't that we can understand everything God has written; much less know how it applies to ourselves. But God helps us. "In the sacred books the Father who is in heaven *meets his children* with great love and *speaks with them.*" We aren't just dealing with written words; God is a living teacher. Jesus promised that "the Advocate, the Holy Spirit, whom the Father will send in my name, will teach you everything, and remind you of all that I have said to you." Discipleship owes more to prayer than to pondering. But they go together.

Luke 16:19-31 shows us a man who truly did "trust in human beings"—and in all that humans can have and do. He was rich. He thought it was a blessing. And took it for granted—so much so he wasn't bothered at all by the poor man lying at his gate. He hardly noticed him. The beggar belonged to a different world; not on the same level as his own. This gives us the definition of "rich."

The "rich" are not those who have money, but those who think money entitles them. To more respect. To more voice in affairs. To easier access. To better treatment, even when it has no price tag. (The price tag is on *them*; that is what draws the favors). These are dangerously rich. They are "cursed."

Plenty of rich don't see themselves this way at all. They are not rich; not in the Scriptural sense. The sign of it is their concern for others.

To "love your neighbor as yourself" means to value all people as much as yourself—and those in your social class. It means to feel their needs as your own. To want to help. To live in gratitude, not complacency. Truth helps.

Initiative: Trust truth. Don't run from it. Seek it. In God's word.

March 25, 2011

Feast of the Annunciation

The *Responsorial* (*Psalm* 40) is: *"Here am I, Lord, I come to do your will."*

The Church applies to Mary the promise made to Ahaz in **Isaiah 7:10-14**: "The Lord himself will give you this sign: the young woman [literally "virgin"] shall be with child and bear a son..."

> The basic meaning of the sign in biblical thought is the symbol which indicates the existence or the presence of that which it signifies; it directs the attention to the reality signified.[1]

The Church is the "symbol," the "sacrament," which indicates the existence and presence of Jesus on earth. And calls attention to him.[2]

Whenever he is asked for a sign, Jesus says emphatically that "no sign" will be given but the "sign of Jonah." Except once. When asked to send "manna from heaven," he promised the Eucharist.[3]

The risen body of Jesus was a sign to those who saw him, and is still a sign to those who see him present in Eucharist. Since Jesus' ascension into heaven, the "sign of Jonah" is the Church, the visible body of Jesus risen and active in his members.

The Church, Eucharist, and Mary are the kind of sign that "indicates the presence of that which it signifies." Mary was this to Elizabeth:

> Why has this happened to me, that the mother of my Lord comes to me? For as soon as I heard the sound of your greeting, the child in my womb leaped for joy.[4]

And this is the sign we should be.

Jesus is present in us. "The virgin shall bear a son, and shall name him Emmanuel"—which means, "God with us." As long as Jesus lives in his body on earth, he is "with us." We are his embodied presence.

His presence is visible through our lifestyle. However we live, Jesus wants to reveal himself living with us, in us, and through us. Our way of living, acting, and speaking should be the sign that reveals the presence of Jesus in us.

Whatever we do, Jesus wants to do it with us, in us, and through us. Wherever we go, he wants to go with us, be in us, and act through us. Everyone who encounters us should encounter Jesus along with us, present in us, speaking through us. As "soon as they hear the sound of our voice," they should feel, whether conscious of its source or not, something within them "leap for joy." Does this sound crazy?

In **Hebrews 10:4-10** Jesus says, "a body you have prepared for me." We are that body. At every moment the passionate thrust of our heart should be, *"Here am I, Lord, I come to do your will."*

Whatever God asks or allows to happen to us, we answer with Mary in **Luke 1:26-38**, "Let it be with me according to your word." Then we are the sign of Jonah." We are "Emmanuel."[5]

[1]John McKenzie, *Dictionary of the Bible*, "Sign."
[2]See *Vatican II*, "The Church," no. 1; *Catechism of the Catholic Church*, nos. 770-776, 1108.
[3]*Matthew* 12:39; 16:4; *Mark* 8:12; *Luke* 11:29; *John* 2:18-22; 6:22-59.
[4]*Luke* 1:39-45.
[5]The classic book by Pierre De Caussade, S.J., *Abandonment to Divine Providence*, makes this the sum and substance of the whole spiritual life.

Initiative: Imagine the Hail Mary addressed to you. What adaptations are needed?

(SAME DAY)

The *Responsorial* (*Psalm* 105) gives a simple remedy to many troubles: *"Remember the marvels the Lord has done."* If we pay attention to the *Liturgy of the Word* we will hear enough of those marvels to be able to remember some when we need to.

Genesis 37:3-28 shows us what envy can do. And what God can do in spite of it. Envy is more than jealousy. Jealousy is to want something another has. Envy is to hate so much the fact the other has something I don't that I don't want the other to have it either.

Joseph's brothers were envious. They hated the fact he enjoyed more love from their father than they did. Enough to stop it by killing him. But they weren't completely evil. Reuben delayed the killing, hoping to rescue Joseph. Judah suggested slavery rather than slaughter. And God worked through the good in both of them.

He worked so well, and things turned out so well for Joseph and his whole family, that it comes to mind when we *"Remember the marvels the Lord has done."* It gives hope in time of trouble.

Envy often makes us lose, or keeps us from getting, the very thing we want. In **Matthew 21:33-46** the point of Jesus' story is that by being envious of his power and popularity with the people, who "regarded him as a prophet," the "chief priests and Pharisees" were going to lose whatever power and prestige they had. In the story, the tenant farmers had a pretty good life and could have kept it if envy and greed had not moved them to kill the owner's son. By killing him they lost everything.

Envy and jealousy have no place in the Church. Among those doing the work of the Kingdom, there are no competitors; just allies. This includes other Catholics and also Protestants whose gifts, projects, and approaches are different from ours. Jesus said, "whoever is not against you is for you."[1]

Here again we find the *Liturgy of the Word* recalling us to truth—or to the truth of the whole picture. We get so caught up in things we are passionate about, that we need the Mass readings—readings chosen for us, not by us—to break us out of our tunnel vision and broaden our perspective. It is a wise thing to do, whenever we have difficulty with another's zeal, to ask (with interest, not challenge) what words of Jesus fire that zeal. If we can agree on their meaning, we have a common basis of understanding, even if we disagree about some details. All religious dialogue should start with what we agree on.

A further step is to ask how the other felt moved by grace, by the Spirit, to live out God's word in this particular way. We may find we have both had similar experiences of receiving and discerning inspirations of the Spirit. Then we are united in the "communion of the Holy Spirit." And together we can *"Remember the marvels the Lord has done."*

[1]*Luke 9:50*

Initiative: Notice envy. Turn it to good by reaching a level of shared blessing.

March 26, 2011

The *Responsorial* (*Psalm* 103) gives a hope in God's love that encourages conversion. *"The Lord is kind and merciful."*

Micah 7:14-20 tells us that if we feel blocked from Mass or from participation in the sacraments, the block is not because of God's attitude.

We may think it is. We may think that God—or the Church—does not accept us. That God's acceptance is conditional on our "living up" to some law or ideal we are not able—or, to be honest, perhaps just not willing—to live up to. We feel blocked from Confession (Reconciliation) because we don't have the "firm purpose of amendment" we may have learned in religion class was necessary to receive absolution.

If we think this, what we didn't learn in religion class was what God is really like. We get that best directly from the word of God. Micah says, for starters, that God is different from anyone we have ever known or heard of: "Who is there like you?" And what does Micah focus on that is different? "The God who removes guilt and pardons sin...."

Who are we to say God cannot remove our guilt and pardon our sins? Who are we to say what his conditions are? Why do we think God's power to forgive is limited by our power to repent?

Well, it is, isn't it? Confession without sorrow for sin or the intention to do better is hypocrisy. It takes two to tango: God's good will and ours, right?

Right. And wrong. It depends on how you understand it.

In **Luke 15:1-32**, was the "prodigal son" sorry for his sins? All Jesus says is that he was sorry he was hungry! And ready to make a deal. If his father would take him back as a hired hand, he would settle for that.

He admitted that what he did was wrong. "I have sinned against God and against you." Yes, we do have to "come to our senses" enough to call a sin a sin. Rationalization is deadly. But even some sins have a lot of good in them. We can be sorry for the bad without regretting what was good. Or being strong enough to stop.

The son decided to "break away and return." A clean conversion. But what if it is not so simple? What if we can't "break away" entirely? Can we still return? Or do we have to keep starving—and specifically, for Eucharist?

Notice that the father didn't ask any questions. It was enough for him that his son was back. If we return to our Father's house and Mass, do we think he will keep us from the table? If we have enough faith, hope, and love to desire to participate in Eucharist, we can't be completely dead. How will we regain health and strength without being nourished by the "bread of life" that the Church tells us we receive "from the table of *both the word of God and of the body of Christ*"? If we are drawn to our Father's house, we are family. If we are family, we eat. God will bring us to healing. *"The Lord is kind and merciful."* Let him be God.

Initiative: Don't set limits on your desire or God's. Do what you can and let him.

FOR REFLECTION AND DISCUSSION: LENT WEEK TWO

We get so caught up in things in our culture that are important to others—and ourselves—that we need the Mass readings—readings chosen for us, not by us—to break us out of our tunnel vision and broaden our perspective.

Invitation: To keep assembling with the community for Mass and *listening* during the *Liturgy of the Word* so that truth will catch up with us, whether or not we want to hear it.

Ask yourself in prayer and others in discussion, for each statement below: Do you see this in the Scripture reading? What response does it invite?

Sunday: If we want a motivating goal for our life, we need to keep striving to make the *event* of Christ's death and resurrection the explanation for everything we do.

Our glory is to "be Christ." And his glory is to be manifestly alive and risen in us.

Monday: What limits God is our refusal to open ourselves. If we close our minds, God cannot enlighten us as he wants. If we close our hearts, God cannot love through us as he will. If we refuse to forgive, God cannot give us his peace.

Tuesday: The *Liturgy of the Word* is part of every Mass to ensure we have direct exposure to God's words. Secondhand discipleship is deficient and dangerous.

We need to obey every legitimate authority, but as disciples, not dumbbells. We should view all opinions and optional customs in the light of the word of God.

Wednesday: We should shun *power* for ourselves and mistrust it in others.

Change is in the air. And the air is the Spirit of God. Every identified abuse is the first blossom of reform.

Thursday: The "rich" are not those who have money, but those who think their money, position, or power entitles them.

Friday: Jealousy is to want something another has. Envy is to hate so much the fact the other has something I don't that I don't want the other to have it either.

Among those doing the work of the Kingdom, there are no competitors; just allies.

All religious dialogue should start with what we agree on. We should root every discussion in shared and recognized, mutual experience of God.

Saturday: We need to call a sin a sin, because rationalization is deadly. But some sins also have good in them. We can be sorry for the bad without denying the good.

Decisions:

Listen to the readings. Measure yourself by what you hear.

Expect some errors in "ordinary" teaching and practice. Try to fix them.

Trust truth. Don't run from it. Seek it with an open mind in God's word.

Never read the Scriptures without active faith, hope, and love.

MARCH 27, 2011
The Pace of Conversion

INVENTORY

Do I ever get discouraged about growing into intimate friendship with God? Am I tempted, because of my sins or shortcomings, to stop reading Scripture and praying? When I feel like this, how does God feel?

INPUT

The *Entrance Antiphon* encourages us to believe God is *always* working to set us free from whatever holds us back from him: *"My eyes are ever fixed on the Lord, for he releases my feet from the snare."* God says, *"I will prove my holiness through you"*—his love, his mercy, and power—by *"gathering you from the ends of the earth. I will pour clean water on you and wash away all your sins. I will give you a new spirit within you."*

Is this a good reason to persevere? God accepts gradual conversion. So should we. All he asks is "forward motion." And so in the *Opening Prayer* we pray, "When we are discouraged by *our weakness*, give us confidence in *your love.*"

THE VOICES WE HEAR

The *Responsorial* (*Psalm* 95) alerts us to the different "voices that cry in the desert." *If today you hear his voice, harden not your hearts.* There is God's voice and there are other voices that come from our own predispositions, from the influence of the culture, or even from the devil. How do we know which is which?

Exodus 17:3-7 warns us to be suspicious of any voice that leads toward discouragement or suggests doubt about God's love, God's reliability, God's readiness to help us. The going was getting tough in the desert. The people were beginning to doubt they would ever reach the Promised Land. They were tempted to go back to the life they had left: security at the price of slavery. They complained to Moses: "Why did you ever make us leave Egypt?" What voice were they listening to?

It is characteristic of God to encourage, not discourage; to build up, not tear down. So the minute we notice that a train of thought is blocking our forward motion, leading us toward discouragement or less confidence in God's love for us, we need to reject it. When a voice says, "You are just proud and delusional. What makes you think God would ask anything great of you? Be realistic. Be humble and settle for an ordinary, mediocre life. You are no *disciple!*"—that is the time to "sing joyfully to the Lord," to "acclaim the Rock of our salvation" and dream great dreams, trusting not in what we are, but in what God is.

THE BASIS OF HOPE

Romans 5:1-8 roots our reason for hope in the fact that God took flesh in Jesus and chose to die for us "while we were still weak." Paul's argument is, "Perhaps for a good person someone might actually dare to die. But God proves his love for us in that while we still were sinners Christ died for us."

If the worst sins we ever committed did not stop Jesus from dying for us, do we think the sins we are committing now will make him stop pouring out his grace on us? Having died to win us to himself, will he give up when it looks like he is losing us?

The problem is, when we feel discouraged, we look at ourselves and our failings instead of looking at Jesus and his love.

What characterizes God's love is *fidelity* or steadfastness. The words Moses heard when God "showed him his glory" were: "a God merciful and gracious, slow to anger, and abounding in *steadfast love and faithfulness*" (*Exodus* 33:12 to 34:6). If we think more about what God *is* and less about what we are *not*, we will find the way out of discouragement.

JESUS THE FISHERMAN

John 4:5-42 shows us how Jesus interacts with sinners. He initiates a conversation with a Samaritan woman he meets at the village well. (For the Jews the Samaritans were like heretics). He begins by asking her for a drink of water. Then, little by little he gets deeper and more personal with her. When she tells him she has no husband, Jesus answers, "You are right, for you have had five husbands, and the one you have now is not your husband." But he gives her credit: "What you have said is true!"

Was Jesus judging her? The only obvious judgment he made was that she was worth talking to, and that she was able to respond to him with faith. And before the day was over, "many Samaritans from that city believed in him because of the woman's testimony."

Conversion to Jesus—or deeper conversion to Jesus—can begin at any point in our lives, and it does not have to be immediately whole and entire. There is no record that Jesus even asked the woman he met to stop living with the man to whom she was not married. Maybe she wasn't ready for that. Nor did he ask the Samaritans to give up their false beliefs. He accepted them as they were and was willing to work with them. The point he made to his disciples was, "Look around you, and see how the fields are ripe for harvesting!" They should focus, not on people's sins, but on their potential. The role of his disciples is not to drive people away but to draw them in. This means accepting them as they are.

To accept others as they are, we have to believe that Jesus accepts *us* as *we* are.

DIRECT DISCIPLESHIP

The *Liturgy of the Word* puts us into direct, immediate contact with the inspired word of God. We don't claim that everything in the Gospels is a direct quote from Jesus: each evangelist wrote from a particular point of view, intent on leading us to particular insights, using various sources. As one teacher put it, "See each Gospel as a *meditation* on the event of Jesus."

The difference between the Gospels and anyone else's meditation is that God says about the Gospels, "This is *my* meditation." God's point of view is always the right one, if we can discern what it is. And in the different Gospels he presents the Good News from various points of view, all of them reliable.[1]

Other people's meditations on the Good News—or their interpretations of the inspired meditations in the Gospels—are only more or less reliable. This includes—are you ready for a shock?—some viewpoints that have been passed down to us through the ages as "the teaching of the Church."

The authentic teaching of the Church is always true, always reliable (if we understand and interpret it right). But not all the teachings *in* the Church are teachings *of* the Church. The bishops at the Second Vatican Council warned us that "believers can have more than a little to do with the rise of atheism"— and even more so with the widespread defection from the Church we see today:

> To the extent that they are careless about their instruction in the faith, or present its teaching falsely, or even fail in their religious, moral, or social life, they must be said to conceal rather than to reveal the true nature of God and of religion.

This is true of both official and non-official teachers. Even the "ordinary *magisterium*" of the Church is by definition not "infallible." Recognizing this,

> this Council urges *all concerned* to remove or correct any abuses, excesses, or defects which may have crept in here or there, and so restore all things that Christ and God be more fully praised.[2]

"All concerned" means every Christian. That is why it is essential that we all keep drinking from the pure spring of God's own words—if for no other reason than to raise fruitful questions in our minds to which we can seek more careful answers. The *Liturgy of the Word* encourages us to do this.

[1]See the explanation of myths as "God's stories" in the reflection above on *Genesis* 1:1-19 for Monday of the Fifth Week of the Year.
[2]Austin Flannery, *Vatican II*, "The Church in the Modern World," no. 19, and "The Church," no. 51.

Insight:
Do I focus more on what blocks me—or others—from full relationship with Jesus, or on what there is in me—and in them—to work with?

Initiative:
Decide never to let any sin or failing block you from interacting with Jesus in every way that is possible for you here and now.

MARCH 28, 2011

The *Responsorial* (*Psalms* 42 and 43) is: *"My soul is thirsting for the living God. When shall I see him face to face?"*

In **Kings 5:1-15** the mistake Naaman made was that he had some prior expectations about how a "prophet" would act. When Elisha did not "come out, invoke the Lord, and move his hand over the spot" where his leprosy was, he lost whatever faith he had in his ability to help him. He wouldn't even follow the simple direction, "Go and wash seven times in the Jordan."

Fortunately, he let his servants talk sense to him. "If the prophet had told you to do something extraordinary, would you not have done it? So what do you lose?" Naaman did what he was told, and was cured. But we don't and aren't.

On the Ninth Sunday of the Year (March 6 above) you read:

> Being a disciple means doing something; down-to-earth and daily, like putting a Bible on the pillow where we will have to pick it up at least once a day, and beginning to actually read it.

Did you do that? The same suggestion was made last year, for this same day: To be a disciple, begin small:

> Get a copy of the Bible, a cheap one you are not afraid to write in and underline. Don't put it on a table. Put it on your *pillow....* And tell God you will read *one line* every night before you go to bed.

If you didn't do that (and assuming you are not reading the Bible every day already), was your reason the same as Naaman's? No "signs and wonders" accompanied the suggestion? It didn't sound exotic or "mystical" enough to promise any significant effect on your life? So you treated it as unimportant?

What might you have gained if you had done it? So why not do it now?

People make this same mistake all the time. They even made it with Jesus! In **Luke 4:24-30** the people he grew up with wouldn't believe this "hometown boy" could be the Messiah. He wasn't "different" enough—at least, not in the way they expected him to be.

Have we made our churches places people are too much "at home" in? Should we make them less "user friendly"? More intimidating? Forbid laity to enter the sanctuary? Require fasting, even from water, for several hours before Communion? Insist people dress up for Mass? Put everything into a special language nobody understands? Make children afraid to open their mouths in church?

It might "work." But would it be Christian? Jesus could have acted so divine no one would believe he was human. Instead, he acted so human they found it hard to believe he was divine.

Maybe the answer is to stop depending on appearances and learn to see with the eyes of faith. Let faith tell us what we see instead of letting what we see determine what we believe. Isn't that the core experience of Eucharist?

"My soul is thirsting for the living God. When shall I see him face to face?" The answer is, "Whenever you accept to find him where he is."

Initiative: Do something unimpressive. For starters, put the Bible on your pillow!

MARCH 29, 2011

The *Responsorial* (*Psalm* 25) is: *"Remember your mercies, O Lord."*

During Lent the first reading and the Gospel are chosen to match. The *Responsorial* gives us the theme of both.

The Gospel is going to talk about a man in an impossible situation. To match it, **Daniel 3:25-43** describes a situation the whole People are in that doesn't offer any ray of hope—except God:

> For we are reduced, O Lord, beyond any other nation, brought low in the world this day because of our sins. We have in our day no prince, prophet, or leader.

What hope is there for a nation—or a church—that seems to be losing on every level? No competent authorities or government ("no prince"); no one inspired by God to lift up a voice in prophetic witness about the situation ("no prophet"); and no private individuals willing and able to take the initiative for reform ("no leader").

Were things as bad as Daniel said? God certainly inspired him to describe the situation as he saw it. But that was just the setting for the real message:

> We follow you unreservedly; for those who trust in you cannot be put to shame.... Deal with us in your kindness and great mercy.... And bring glory to your name, O Lord!

Do we sometimes feel that Daniel's description fits the Church? If so, we have a very small field of vision. Even with all the defects and defections we can identify, there are throughout the Church dynamic communities and parishes, initiatives, and movements inspired and empowered by the Spirit. One only has to look to see.

This, however, only leads to optimism. And optimism, even well-founded, is not hope. Optimism is a human judgment based on our perception of human abilities and activity. Hope is divine assurance based on the nature of God. Optimists expect something to happen, usually within a time-frame. They can be disappointed. Those who hope in God know something is already happening, but not when it will become evident. They are never disappointed.

God is not an optimist. But **Matthew 18:21-35** teaches us God never fails to hope in our ability to convert to him and "pay back in full" the gift of existence through eternal praise and thanksgiving. We may not actually do it, but God knows we can. God keeps loving us and giving us the grace to do it until our choice is sealed in death.

Jesus teaches that we must love one another as he does, with God's own "steadfast love," because we share in God's divine life. We can never give up on anyone on earth whom God is still choosing to will into existence, because that is to give up on God.

The same holds true for us. When we are "brought low in the world... because of our sins," we tend to think that what has happened to us through our own choices can only be reversed through our own efforts. We feel like the debtor in Jesus' story whose resources were hopelessly insufficient to save him. But God has unlimited resources. We just have to ask him to use them. *"Remember your mercies, O Lord."*

Initiative: Measure everything by God—whose borders are out of sight.

MARCH 30, 2011

Why does the *Responsorial* (*Psalm* 147) invite us: *"Praise the Lord, Jerusalem"*?

Deuteronomy 4:1-9 says God's laws are so good and just that if we live by them people will say, "This great nation is truly a wise and intelligent people."

We would be, if we had written them. But since they were given to us by God, we can only claim credit for being smart enough to recognize how good they are. And the jury is still out on whether we are that smart or not.

Have you ever given thought to how wise God's laws are? How much sense it makes to live by them? How they enhance our life on earth?

Most of us weren't taught to do this. Our teachers may have thought it would be motivation enough just to know these are God's commands. But it isn't.

When you confess a sin in Confession, does the priest ever ask you, "Why does God command (or forbid) that?" Do you ever ask the question yourself?

Some unenlightened teachers discourage questioning, especially about religion. But God is disappointed if we do not question everything he tells us. Christianity, the religion of "God-made-human," calls us to be always, as much as possible, "fully human and fully divine." We know by divine faith that God is always right. But God wants us to know it with our human intelligence as well. Theology (study of the "logos" or intelligibility of God) is defined as "faith seeking understanding." That is a good definition of *discipleship*.

Deuteronomy urges us emphatically to life-long discipleship: "Take care, be earnestly on your guard not to forget." We should not allow to "slip from memory" the things we have learned from teachers, from reflection on God's word, from experience, as "long as we live." The Scripture says, "Teach them to your children and to your children's children." We ourselves should teach them. This is the word of God.

In **Matthew 5:17-19** Jesus gives the key to the New Law he teaches in the "Sermon on the Mount" (*Matthew*, chapters 5-7): "I have come, not to abolish the law and the prophets, but to fulfill them." The Law enhances life. Jesus came that we might "have life, and have it to the full." So his New Law fulfills or "fills full" the old. How?

In a word, by changing the goal. The Commandments are the "manufacturer's instructions" for getting the most here on earth out of the human nature God designed for us. If we live by them, even the "nations" will see us as a "wise and intelligent people." People who know how to live on this earth.

But the New Law gives guidelines for living on the level of God. "Those who fulfill and teach these commands" will not just earn respect as good human beings. They "shall be great in the kingdom of God." That is, in the milieu of those who live by the divine life of God, directed from within by the mind and heart of God, which has become their own. *"Praise the Lord!"*

Initiative: Challenge everything—not to doubt, but to understand.

MARCH 31, 2011

The *Responsorial* (*Psalm* 95) is a survival principle: *"If today you hear his voice, harden not your hearts."*

God tells **Jeremiah (7:23-28)** that from the day the people left Egypt until now he has "sent untiringly" prophets to guide them. But they won't listen. And, "when you speak… they will not listen to you either!" Do we?

Isn't God's word constantly available to us? Can't we pick up the Bible any time we want? Aren't the "prophets" preaching every Sunday? Every day, even, for those at daily Mass? Don't children have parents and teachers, and all of us friends God uses to help us? Do we listen?

God's conclusion is sobering: "Faithfulness has disappeared. The word itself is banished from their speech."

The word is "commitment." How often is it used? Does it stop divorces? Does the commitment of Baptism (the most radical in human life) stop people from giving up Mass, leaving the Church? Are we conscious of breaking our commitment, our covenant with God, when we sin? God's self-description is "steadfast love." Is "steadfast" the word that characterizes our pledged love?

It could be. Would be, God suggests, if we would just *"Listen* to my voice." If we would just read God's word with open minds and hearts, everything could be different for us. Discipleship "works."

In **Luke 11:14-23** Jesus identifies another problem; the root problem, really.

The Scriptural word for it is "idolatry," which we no longer understand.

"Idolatry" means dividedness. It is the contrary of the First Commandment:

> Hear, O Israel: The LORD is our God, the LORD alone. You shall love the LORD your God with *all* your heart, and with *all* your soul, and with *all* your might.

"All" means all. One hundred percent. Nothing left over. If we are committed to God as God—to the One God as "Lord alone"—we have made an all-inclusive choice. No other choices can call it into question. Anything that does is an "idol." A false god. A created value we have made comparable, even if not equal, to God. Comparable enough for us to compare them and choose between them. If "Thy will be done" is not absolute for us; if it does not pre-determine every choice, we are idolaters. To some degree, we all are.

God's answer was to send his Son. The practical answer to idolatry is to make an idol of Jesus: but a true one. Christianity "works" if we make the person of Jesus our abiding focus. Religion itself can offer idols. We can divide our devotion between various doctrines, laws, and practices. We can lose Jesus by focusing on prayers to say, devotions to follow, practices to observe. We can be loyal or disloyal to popes, priests, and bishops without connecting to Jesus. They can command and preach without referring to him. This gives "aid and comfort" to idolatry. Jesus says, "whoever does not gather with me scatters." *"If today you hear his voice, harden not your hearts."*

Initiative: **Narrow your focus** to Jesus. Then broaden it to include everything else.

APRIL 1, 2011

The *Responsorial* (*Psalm* 81) is incomprehensible: "*I am the Lord your God: hear my voice.*"

It is impossible to summarize these readings—just as it is impossible to begin to grasp what "*I am the Lord your God*" means. We could sit silent in front of that mystery for the rest of our lives.

So read **Hosea 14:2-10**. Then re-read it. Then read the *Responsorial Psalm*—all of it. Then start over. Read **Mark 12:28-34**. It is saying the same thing. Keep reading until you realize you don't understand any of it and yet have grasped the meaning of all of it.

Then sit in silent wonder before your God.

"*Return....*" What does it mean that God says this? Not just a human; God himself. What depth and breadth and length and height does it contain?

"Say to him, '*Forgive all iniquity.*'" Who is saying this to whom? Who is he, that we dare, are encouraged, to say it? Who is this God we are dealing with?

"*We shall say no more, 'Our god,' to the work of our hands.*" With "steadfast love" we will work against the idolatry of our hearts embodied in the "work of our hands." In what we do. But if we say it, we need to mean it. At least mean that we will sincerely and perseveringly try. We don't bandy words with God.

How long do we have to think about that before it gets real? Our culture has removed the labels from our idols. They go by legitimate names. What reveals them as idols? As idols for me?

"*I will heal their defection. I will love them freely.*" What does this mean—when it is God who says it? God doesn't act, heal, or love on our limited level. What does this mean on his level? What does it encourage me to feel? To do?

"*I will be like the dew for Israel... he shall strike root and put forth shoots.*" We have to read *Psalm 1*. God is talking about *disciples*: those who "*meditate day and night.*"

> They are like trees planted by streams of water, which yield their fruit in its season, and their leaves do not wither. In all that they do, they prosper.

Do these words mean anything to you? What have they inspired you to do? Have you grasped their meaning, under the imagery? Have you really? Do you really believe what they say?

You don't unless you are doing it. Are you meditating? "Let those who are wise *understand these things.* Let those who are prudent *know them.*"

Look up what "know" means in Scripture. It means to get in bed with. To touch every part of. To lose yourself in. To possess totally in total surrender.

Do you "know these things"? If not, become a *disciple*.

> This book of the law shall not depart out of your mouth; you shall meditate on it day and night, so that you may be careful to act in accordance with all that is written in it. For then you shall make your way prosperous, and then you shall be successful (*Joshua* 1:8).

"*I am the Lord your God: hear my voice.*"

Initiative: Be awed. Stand before the mystery of God. Let it fill you.

APRIL 2, 2011

The *Responsorial* (*Hosea* 6:6 and *Psalm* 51) says God wants us to *know* him: *"It is steadfast love, not sacrifice, that God desires."* The verse continues: *"...the knowledge of God* rather than burnt offerings." God wants *disciples*.

Hosea 6:1-6 shows us the predictable path of discipleship.

The starting point, as often as not, is seeking an escape from pain. *"In their affliction they shall look for me."*

When we are "in the pits," all we want is a return to ground level: a basically human, reasonable way of life. We want God to "heal" our human natures and "revive" us, as in "re-vivify," make us alive again. We have hope that God will.

But our hope is focused on healing: restoring the level of life we received at creation, from which we "fall short" by following appetites, emotions, and the culture instead of reason. (The common Scriptural word for sin is *hamartia*: to "miss the mark"). We want God to "raise us up, to live in his presence," because sin is separation from the Good, the True, and the Beautiful that are found in God as Creator, the truth that clarifies our own being; the goodness that puts order into everything we do. Whose rejection is disorder. As long as we are "in the pits" we cannot focus on God in himself; we go to God to escape pain. That is why most people went to Jesus.

But once out of the pits and restored to ground level we can begin to "lift up our eyes to the mountain." Now, feeling the intrinsic longing of our human nature for the "more," we say, *"Let us know, let us strive to know the Lord."*

This is a distinct and very important phase of discipleship. Now we are able to look at God just in order to know him. We can hear God's words without immediately focusing them on our human needs. Now we can be students of God's mind and heart.

This activates another level of hope: hope in *enlightenment* for its own sake; that is, for the sake of knowing Truth and Goodness as such; for the sake of knowing God. We may struggle with the discipline of discipleship, and feel discouraged when prayer and reflection seem fruitless. But our new hope tells us, *"Certain as the dawn is his coming."* We await him like "the light of day," with hope that he will *"come to us like... spring rain that waters the earth."* We hope for *union* with him whose Light is Life: life on the level of God.

Now the focus turns to *perseverance*. God speaks out of his experience of fickle humans: *"Your piety is like a morning cloud, like the dew that passes away."* Discipleship requires commitment. As Woody Allen said about success, "Eighty percent of it is just showing up."

But we need to show up with the right attitude. And the attitude, even to get beyond our needs, is *need*. In **Luke 18:9-14** Jesus tells us "those who humble themselves shall be exalted." Discipleship is not accomplishment. It is begging. With "a heart contrite and humbled."

Initiative: Seek to know God. Seek it with efforts, but receive it as gift.

FOR REFLECTION AND DISCUSSION: LENT WEEK THREE

All God asks is "forward motion." God is always working to set us free from whatever holds us back from him. But God accepts gradual conversion. So should we.

Invitation: Keep drinking from the pure spring of God's own words. They raise fruitful questions in our minds to which we can seek more careful answers.

Ask yourself in prayer and others in discussion, for each statement below: Do you see this in the Scripture reading? What response does it invite?

Sunday: Be suspicious of any voice that leads toward discouragement or suggests doubt about God's love or readiness to help us.

When we feel discouraged, we are looking at ourselves instead of at Jesus. We should think more about what God *is* and less about what we are *not*.

The role of Christ's disciples is not to drive people away but to draw them in. We accept people as they are, and focus, not on their sins, but on their potential.

Monday: Optimism is a human judgment based on our perception of human abilities and activity. Hope is divine assurance based on the nature of God.

We can never give up on anyone on earth whom God is still choosing to will into existence, because that is to give up on God.

Tuesday: Some unenlightened teachers discourage questioning, especially about religion. But God is disappointed if we do not question everything he tells us.

Wednesday: The Commandments are the "manufacturer's instructions" for getting the most out of the human nature God designed for us. But the New Law gives guidelines for living on the level of God.

Thursday: If we are committed to the One God as "Lord alone," we have made an all-inclusive choice. Anything that calls it into question is an "idol."

Friday: If we really believe in God's promises we will do what they call for. If we don't, perhaps we haven't really understood what we believe.

Saturday: As long as we are "in the pits," we cannot focus on God in himself; we go to God to escape pain. That is why most people went to Jesus.

When we can hear God's words without immediately focusing them on our human needs, we can be students of God's mind and heart.

Decisions:

Never let any sin or failing block you from interacting with Jesus in every way that is possible for you here and now.

Challenge everything—not to doubt, but to understand.

Do something unimpressive. For starters, put the Bible on your pillow!

APRIL 3, 2011
Conversion to a New Guidance System

INVENTORY

How do I make most of my decisions? Is it by common sense? By applying rules and doctrines to situations? By reflecting on things in the light of Scripture? By trying to discern the voice of the Holy Spirit in my heart?

INPUT

The *Entrance Antiphon* calls us to rejoice in the Church (the new Jerusalem): "Be glad for her, you who love her; rejoice with her, you who mourned for her, and you will find contentment at her consoling breasts." We may see many faults in the Church to mourn over. But if we love her, we will seek nourishment from her and we will find it. We just have to know where to look. And we have to look with the eyes of faith. This is to use God's guidance system.

In the *Opening Prayer* we declare to the "Father of peace" that we are indeed joyful in our relationship with "your Son Jesus Christ." We follow the Church through the season of Lent and into Easter "with the eagerness of faith and love," knowing that we are being led into the fullness of life.

THROUGH GOD'S EYES:

The *Responsorial* (*Psalm* 23) calls us to believe and affirm with faith that, in spite of all appearances, *"the Lord is our shepherd; there is nothing we shall want."*

1Samuel 16:1-13 teaches us not to judge by appearances: "for the LORD does not see as mortals see; they look on the outward appearance, but the LORD looks on the heart." If we want to be disciples of Jesus, it is not enough to accept what he sees and tells us; we have to learn how to look at things as he does.

There is a learning process here—we have to form the human habit of looking at things as God does—but first and foremost this is a gift of God. It is only by the divine gift of faith that we can share in God's act of knowing. And

this is what Christian insight is: seeing by sharing in what Christ within us sees. To be authentic disciples of Jesus, we have to convert to following a new guidance system: the divine light of God within us instead of the natural light of human reason alone. *The Lord is our shepherd.* If we let him show us truth and guide us, *there is nothing we shall want.*

THE LIGHT OF LIFE:

Ephesians 5:8-14 insists that we must recognize the difference between the guidance of Jesus and the light of this world, which shines through our cultural conditioning and the current trends and values in society. This includes the brilliance of shortsighted intellectuals who, in spite of their impressive knowledge, are blind to what even the natural light of reason could tell them about God. In contrast to them, St. Paul tells believers, "Once you were darkness, but now in the Lord you are light. Live as children of light."

This is not a rejection of human reason. As disciples of God-made-human in Jesus we accept everything human as good. But it is a *transcendence* of the human, a "going beyond" what is merely human, to live and see and act on the level of God. To be disciples of the divine-human Jesus, we have to convert to living lives that are not just human but divine. The Lord is our shepherd; he leads us, not only along "right paths," but to pastures our earthly minds cannot even dream of. He came that we might "have life and have it to the full" (*John* 10:10). But our life, our joy, can only be filled by what addresses our capacity for total truth, total goodness, total love. It is only through the outpouring of the Holy Spirit that our "cup overflows."

LIGHT IN THE WORLD

An underlying theme of **John 9:1-41** is that the light of God is available *on earth*, and we come into it through down-to-earth human actions. When Jesus opened the eyes of the man born blind, he "spat on the ground and made mud with the saliva and spread the mud on the man's eyes." This is so earthy it shocks us; we would expect something more hygienic from God! Then he told the man, "Go, wash in the pool of Siloam." There wasn't going to be any miracle until the man took a bath.

All this was to emphasize that we open ourselves to the divine by doing human things. We interact with a very human Church. We listen with our ears, read with our eyes, think with our brains, make decisions with our wills, carry them out into action with our hands and feet. God doesn't just turn us on like light bulbs. To come into the light we have to be *disciples*, which means *active learners*.

John said, "The true light, which enlightens everyone, was coming into the *world*" (*John* 1:9). Jesus comes from above, but we meet him on ground level. We find him in "word and sacrament," by gathering with other physical bodies for worship, through serious engagement with Jesus enlightening us through preachers, teachers, and discussion groups.

The once-blind man asked the Pharisees, "Do you also want to become his disciples?" That is the question this Gospel asks us. How will I answer?

INSIGHT
What human things do I need to do in order to open myself more to the divine light of Christ? How can I use my eyes, ears, mouth, hands, and feet?

INITIATIVE:
Get specific about how you will seek encounter with Christ through "word and sacrament." How will you use Scripture, Eucharist, Confession? How will you look for Christ in the Christian community? Through what kind of interaction?

APRIL 4, 2011

The *Responsorial* (*Psalm* 30) is an acknowledgement each one of us needs to make. Frequently. *"I will praise you, Lord, for you have rescued me."*

What kind of God comes through in **Isaiah 65:17-21?**

> Lo, I am about to create new heavens and a new earth.... There shall always be rejoicing and happiness in what I create. For I create Jerusalem [read "the Church"] to be a joy, and its people to be a delight.

Larry, a Baptist minister, told at a dinner party how his loving wife was the one who kept order in the family. She got their daughter Jane off to school, regulated the TV, and kept the candy down. But Larry didn't conform: "I just gave Jane everything she wanted."

One morning, when his wife left for a trip, Jane said, "I don't want to go to school today." "Great," Larry laughed, "Let's take a holiday!" The other mothers at the table all looked horrified as he told how they just stayed home for the rest of the week. Watched television. Ate junk food. Had a ball.

Before his wife's return Larry suggested to Jane, "You know, there are some things mommy doesn't need to hear."

Isn't the Church like a mother to us? Loving, but conscientious. Mothers set the rules. They keep family life ordered. It is necessary. But it isn't the whole picture.

Can you see God the Father acting like this Baptist minister? One Sunday you wake up, see glorious weather outside, and say to the Father, "I don't want to go to

Mass today." Can you imagine God the Father laughing and saying, "Fine! Let's take a holiday!" And making sure you have one of the most enjoyable days of your life?

Do you see disapproving glances among those who read this? But wouldn't you guess Jane did not follow the rebellious "minister's daughter syndrome" when she became adult? Wouldn't you bet she is still going to church?

Please don't tell anybody what you read here. There are some things everybody doesn't need to hear!

How does Jesus come through in **John 4:43-54?** According to the "rules" the official didn't qualify for a miracle. Jesus' standard remark to those he cured was: "Your faith has made you well.... According to your faith let it be done to you." Jesus reproached the official for lacking it: "Unless you people see signs and wonders, you do not believe."

But the official saw in Jesus more than someone who lived by rules, even his own! He appealed directly to Christ's heart, the law of all laws, to the love that gives life: "Sir, come down before my child dies." Jesus said, "Return home. Your son will live." Then he believed. In Christ's love.

> The man believes "the word spoken to him." ...He had [not] acquired perfect faith, but it was a beginning.... The cure appears to be not so much the cause of the man's faith [as] its consequence; signs and faith in the word go together. [1]

Love won his faith. Hearing God's word with faith in his love is *discipleship.*

[1] See *Matthew* 9:22-29; 17:20; 21:21-22; *John* 10:10; 21:15-18; *Jerome Biblical Commentary,* 1968.

Initiative: Obey the rules, but... interpret them according to the Father's heart.

TUESDAY FOURTH WEEK IN LENT

APRIL 5, 2011

The *Responsorial* (*Psalm* 46) tells us to trust: *"The mighty Lord is with us; the God of Jacob is our refuge."*

Ezekiel 47:1-12 is about water, a symbol of the life God gives in Baptism. All who have this life within them should be sources of life for others: "Wherever the river flows, every living creature that can multiply shall live."

Picture it: a clean, flowing river. On both banks, green plants, flowers, crops, and trees. This is the way the world should look, wherever Christians are. At least to those who have eyes to see the Life God gives. "I appointed you to go and bear fruit, fruit that will last."

Jesus used this same image with the woman of Samaria: "If you knew the gift of God, and who it is that is saying to you, 'Give me a drink,' you would have asked him, and he would have given you living water." Later he said: "Out of the believer's heart shall flow rivers of living water." Those who receive life are to give life.

John continues: "Now he said this about the Spirit, which believers in him were to receive." Jesus had said, "It is the spirit that gives life... The words that I have spoken to you are spirit and life."[1]

The "daily way" to receive and increase God's life within us—and transmit it to others—is to read God's *words*, praying for enlightenment by his Holy Spirit. To do this regularly is to be a *disciple*. In every Mass the *Liturgy of the Word* reminds and calls us to this. What this reading does is give us motivation: by opening ourselves to the "water of life" by reflecting on God's words, we will become fountains of life for others. Is that worth investing time in?

John 5:1-16 ends with the sobering statement: "It was because Jesus did such things on the Sabbath that they began to persecute him." We want to scream: "What things? Healing a sick man? Anyone who would persecute a person for that is the one who is sick!"

But it happens every day. Who within the Church gets persecuted the most by others in the Church, laity as well as officials? Isn't it the "prophets"—those who upset complacency by acting or speaking in a way that calls our assumptions into question?

What did you think of yesterday's reflection? "It was bad, dangerous! It said it's okay to miss Mass on Sunday!"

Is that all you saw? Or did you see God as a wise, loving Father who will dispense with a rule at times to help someone love the Mass and him more? Any priest can dispense from Mass for a good reason. Do we need an authority to make that judgment for us? Or can we look at God's heart and make it for ourselves? The answer to that question is the "litmus test" of Phariseeism.

If the comfortable are afflicted by what comforts the afflicted, they have a problem. It is probably fear of human freedom exercised in decisions.

[1]*John* 4:10; 6:63; 7:37-39; 15:16.

Initiative: Remember: *"The mighty Lord is with us."* Trust God to lead.

APRIL 6, 2011

The *Responsorial* (*Psalm* 145) reminds us *"The Lord is kind and merciful."*

Phariseeism feeds on fear. And a sense of rejection. And unacknowledged anger at not feeling loved. We don't say, but we feel, "The Lord has forsaken me; my Lord has forgotten me." Without the intimacy of personal interaction with God, we fall back on the impersonal relationship of rules. We will "save ourselves" without his help. We will keep the rules so strictly that our "righteousness" will be our revenge.

"Phariseeism" is legalism: a focus on rules with desire to enforce them for others. It is never joyful, never nurturing, never loving. There is always underlying anger in it. And unconscious resentment, which surfaces in anger against those who are not rule-bound. Paul fought the "false believers" who "slipped in to spy on the freedom we have in Christ Jesus, so that they might enslave us."[1]

Isaiah 49:8-15 counters this by describing God's closeness and saving love. "In a time of favor I answer you... I help you." God addresses those whose sense of isolation from him has locked them into the defensive posture of legalism: "Saying to the prisoners: 'Come out!'"... For he who pities them leads them and guides them beside springs of water." Stop focusing on rules. Drink from the spring of God's own heart, revealed in his words. Read. Meditate. Pray. Don't be so afraid. Your fear of sin, in the absence of reliance on God, drives you into the fortress-prison of rigid self-discipline. God will "cut a road" through all that blocks you from him. He has not abandoned you.

> Can a mother forget her infant, be without tenderness for the child of her womb?
>
> Even should she forget, I will never forget you.

In **John 5:17-30** Jesus defends his own freedom against those who persecuted him for healing on the Sabbath. He claims to be acting by a higher law: the law of *union*, of shared life with the Father who acts with him, in him, and through him: "The Son cannot do anything by himself... only what he sees the Father doing"—and doing in him.

More: "Just as the Father possesses life in himself, so has he granted it to the Son to have life in himself." And Jesus can share this life with humans: "The Son grants life to whom he wishes.... The one who hears my word... possesses eternal life."

The *prophets* claim to act by the Light and Life of God within them. They can be deceived. But the worst deception is to deny the prophetic gift entirely and trust in nothing but slavish obedience to laws. This is to deny the faith. By Baptism we share in the life of God. We are anointed, consecrated by God as "priests, prophets, and kings" (responsible stewards of his kingship). The fear that denies freedom to let Christ act *with* us, *in* us, and *through* us is darkness overshadowing faith.

[1] *Galatians* 2:4.

Initiative: Be what you are: alive with the life of God. Act in union with God.

THURSDAY FOURTH WEEK IN LENT

APRIL 7, 2011

The *Responsorial* (*Psalm* 106) presumes the value of prayer: *"Lord, remember us, for the love you bear your people."*

In **Exodus 32:7-14** Moses gives God good advice, reminds him of what God seems to have forgotten, and gets God to change his mind about what he had planned to do. Yeah, right.

This is a good example of the way God inspires the Scripture writers. He inspires them with truth, but truth expressed in the kind of words and images the writers understood, and that the people for whom they were writing would understand. Sometimes a story incorporates assumptions everyone had that were false, but which it was not yet time to challenge.

From our way of seeing things, our prayer does affect what God does. God already knows from all eternity what he is going to do, but he has made some of it conditional on our asking for it. Why?

God does not want to save the world unilaterally. He wants humans to have a part, a real part, in it. One way in our power is to pray for each other. Then God can say, truly, that what he does is our gift as well as his. We ask, God answers, and we are joined in love.

Also, if we "argue" with God, as Moses did, it lets God inspire us with questions and answers that lead us to clearer understanding of ourselves and him. God is a teacher; we are disciples. Disciples learn through dialogue.

In **John 5:31-47** Jesus is trying to dialogue, except that it takes two to tango, and Pharisees never answer.

Jesus gives four reasons for believing in him and seven why people don't.

Bearing witness to Jesus are: 1. *John* the Baptizer, whose life made people trust him; 2. the *works* (good deeds and miracles) Jesus performs; 3. the *Father* himself; 4. the *Scriptures*, and specifically Moses.

People refuse to believe because 1. God's *word* is not abiding in their hearts; 2. and this is because of their free *choice* not to accept Jesus, the "one God has sent"; 3. they don't *desire* eternal life enough to come to Jesus for it; 4. they *accept others* who do not come in the name of God; 5. they *accept praise* from one another; 6. they *do not seek* the glory that comes from God; 7. they *don't believe Moses* or the Scriptures.

Later, Jesus will specify that all the reasons for believing in him are secondary to the testimony the Father and Spirit give within the hearts of those who are open. "Believe me that I am in the Father and the Father is in me; but if you do not, *then believe* me because of the works themselves." Those whose hearts are good will just *know*.[1]

The readings in the *Liturgy of the Word* are intended to encourage *reflection*. So take time to go through the "four and seven" above. See which apply to you.[2]

[1] *John 3:20-21; 6:44-45; 8:42; 10:38; 14:11.*
[2] *General Instruction on the Roman Missal,* no. 56.

Initiative: Believe Scripture as divine revelation. Read it as human dialogue.

APRIL 8, 2011

The *Responsorial* (*Psalm* 34) tells us that, contrary to appearances, *"The Lord is close to the brokenhearted."*

Wisdom 2:1-22 lists four reasons—as common today as then—why some non-believers find those who are authentically religious "obnoxious."

1. Believers "reproach" others for going against God's law. We do. We can't judge others' consciences, but when something is wrong we should say so.

2. Believers "profess to have knowledge of God." Of course. Religion is empty without it. But this is not pride; the knowledge is a gift, not an accomplishment.

3. Believers are "different." The attack here is not consistent with logic. In a religious culture the nonbelievers would be different—and fight for the right to be.

4. Believers "hold aloof from [cultural] paths as from things impure." The question is, "Are they impure?" Unbelievers "hold aloof" from religious services. So?

5. Believers "call blest the destiny of the just." Yes. And since they aren't always "blest" by this world's standards, this calls into question the core values that unbelievers live for. Someone is a fool.

6. Believers "boast that God is their Father." Yes, but it is a gift offered to everyone, not a boast. And its first effect is humility: "O Lord, I am not worthy."

The unbelievers' biggest mistake is to assume God will protect the just from being delivered over to their enemies. Jesus' crucifixion settled that question. But this only makes sense if there is "a recompense of holiness" after death. The bottom line (omitted in the reading) is: "For God created human beings to be immortal; he made them as an image of his own nature." Our stand on that rules our answer to everything else. *"The Lord is close to the brokenhearted."*

An advantage to reading Scripture is that it raises all sorts of questions that are tossed about but not really confronted elsewhere. It helps to confront them, getting help from the word of God.

John 7:1-30: When Jesus calls people to confront the question of his origins—"So you know me...?"—all he explains is, "I was sent." We can like or dislike, understand or misunderstand all sorts of things Jesus teaches. But the only important question is whether God speaks in him. If he does, belief is settled. All that remains is to try to understand, and ask how to put it into practice. That is the work of disciples.

In a theology exam, the first question asked about every Church doctrine and practice is, "Where does it come from?" Scripture? A Church council? The personal viewpoint of a pope, bishop, or scholar? The common consensus of the faithful? Or just unexamined conventional hearsay? To give a doctrine more authority than it has is just as bad as giving it less.

In today's educated Church, every believer is challenged to ask those questions. If we don't, we will become a community of blind led by the blind.

Initiative: Be a responsible believer. Know the origin of what you believe and do.

APRIL 9, 2011

The *Responsorial* (*Psalm* 7) gives us the ruling principle of discipleship: *"O Lord, my God, in you I take refuge."*

The starting point of discipleship is an act of trust in God. Our security is rooted, not in acceptance by others, not in conformity to whatever group in the Church seems most solid and reliable, not even in the approval of popes and bishops, who frequently in history have turned a blind eye to abuses and "stoned the prophets" God sent to them. Our ultimate confidence is in the word of God and carefully discerned enlightenment by the Holy Spirit. To give unqualified trust to anything else, besides the reliable but rare "defined" dogmas of the Church, is idolatry. *"O Lord, my God, in you I take refuge."*[1]

Jeremiah 11:18-20 tells us we don't always know who is speaking or acting against us. "I, like a trusting lamb led to the slaughter, had not realized they were hatching plots against me." It is not paranoia to think that it happens today. A priest "on loan" to an American diocese was denounced in a letter from the bishop's office in his home diocese for sexual misconduct with a consenting adult. The American bishop told his Chancellor to put him on the next plane home. The Chancellor asked if he could check the story first and found proof the letter was a forgery.

Priests and others are frequently denounced to bishops for statements some hearer judged "heretical" (which today almost always means "liberal"). Most bishops simply send the letter to the accused for a response. But some prominent authors and theologians have complained that they were never allowed to confront their accusers or see the actual text of accusations made against them. This is unjust. The right to confront one's accusers is a basic human right.[2]

So what? We live with the truth that we are a sinful, saintly Church. Not to worry. Eventually, God wins. *"O Lord, my God, in you I take refuge."*

In **John 7:40-53** everybody is arguing about the wrong questions—except the temple guards, who when asked why they didn't carry out orders and arrest Jesus, just said, "No man ever spoke like that before." But others argued that he wasn't born in the right place, or accepted by the Sanhedrin (the religious authorities) or by the Pharisees (considered the educated and "fervent"), but only by "this lot, that knows nothing about the law—and they are lost anyway." Nicodemus pointed out it was all irrelevant. "Since when does our law condemn anyone without first knowing both the person and the facts?"

All the false arguments above are still used against controversial figures today. Authentic "disciples" seek to *know Jesus* (and any accused) and *the facts.*

[1]See *Mathew* 5:12; 23:29-39. The worst opponents of Jesus were the established teachers of religion (the "scribes"), the approved "law and order" party (the Pharisees), and the "chief priests." What they all had in common was power and prestige.

[2]Archbishop D'Souza of India accused the Roman Curia of this in *Council Speeches of Vatican II*, edited by Hans Kung, Yves Congar, O.P. and Daniel O'Hanlon, S.J., Deus Books, Paulist Press, 1964, p. 129. Cf. Jefferson: "Eternal vigilance is the price of liberty."

Initiative: Be a disciple of Jesus. Neither accept nor reject without involving Jesus.

FOR REFLECTION AND DISCUSSION: LENT WEEK FOUR

To be authentic disciples of Jesus, we have to convert to following a new guidance system: the divine light of God within us instead of the natural light of human reason alone. This means living lives that are not just human but divine.

Invitation: Jesus offers to "speak peace to a sinful world," and to "teach us," so that "our faith, hope, and love may turn hatred into love, conflict into peace, death into eternal life" and "bring to the human race the gift of reconciliation." If we love what Jesus offers us in the Church and believe in it, we will seek it as *disciples*, as *students* eager to learn and be nourished by God's words.

Ask yourself in prayer and others in discussion, for each statement below: Do you see this in the Scripture reading? What response does it invite?

Sunday: If we love the Church, we will seek nourishment from her and we will find it. We just have to know where to look.

To be disciples of Jesus, it is not enough to accept and do what he tells us. We have to learn how to look at things as he does.

Monday: The Church is like a mother to us: loving, but conscientious. Mothers set the rules, keep family life ordered. It is necessary. But it isn't the whole picture.

Tuesday: Those most persecuted by others in the Church are the "prophets"— those who upset complacency by acting or speaking in a way that calls long-standing assumptions into question.

Wednesday: Without the intimacy of personal interaction with God, we fall back on the impersonal relationship of rules, trying to "save ourselves" without his help.

The worst deception is to deny the prophetic gift out of fear of mistakes and trust in nothing but slavish obedience to laws. This is to deny the faith.

Thursday: God does not want to save the world unilaterally. He wants humans to pray for each other. Then what God does is our gift as well as his.

Friday: In today's educated Church, every believer is challenged to ask about every Church doctrine and practice, "Where does it come from?" If we don't, we will become a community of blind led by the blind.

Saturday: Our ultimate confidence is in the word of God and carefully discerned enlightenment by the Holy Spirit. Unqualified trust in anything else, besides the reliable but rare "defined" dogmas of the Church, is idolatry.

Decisions:

Obey the rules, but interpret them according to the Father's heart.

Believe Scripture as divine revelation. Read it as human dialogue.

Be a responsible believer. Know the origin of what you believe and do.

APRIL 10, 2011

Conversion to Being Divine

INVENTORY

The *Entrance Antiphon* is a prayer of trust: *"Give me justice, O God... Rescue me from the deceitful and the unjust"* (*Psalm* 43). Do I see this happening?

Judging by what I see going on in the world, does it seem that Jesus is winning or losing? Christians believe Jesus triumphed over those who crucified him by being raised by the Father. Do I see any visible evidence of Jesus' resurrection around me today that encourages me to believe in his victory? Am I looking the right way?

INPUT

In the *Opening Prayer* we ask to be like God: "Father, help us to be like Christ your Son." We are the risen body of Jesus on earth. It is in and through us that he is winning the battle against evil today. What do I need to do in order to let him act and win through me?

RESURRECTION IS US:

Ezekiel 37:12-14 does not mention what God will do to his enemies or ours. Ezekiel only speaks of what God will do *for* us: "I will open your graves and have you rise from them.... I will put my spirit in you that you may live." This was the way Jesus triumphed after his crucifixion: he did not obliterate his enemies; he just rose from the dead.

We know Jesus is triumphing in us, not from what we see happening in the world around us, but from what we see happening within ourselves. "I will put my spirit in *you* that *you* may live.... *Thus you shall know* that I am the Lord." We know Jesus is Lord when we experience the "fruit of the Spirit" in our lives. The fruit of the Spirit is love, joy, and peace (see *Galatians* 5:22).

The *Responsorial* (*Psalm* 130) puts our focus on God as giving life, not taking revenge: *"For with the LORD there is steadfast love, and with him is great power to redeem"* (or "fullness of redemption"). God shows his power in saving, in converting, in redeeming, not in condemning and destroying.

This is a lesson the first disciples of Jesus found hard to learn, and we do too. When a Samaritan town would not give Jesus lodging for the night, "his disciples James and John said, 'Lord, do you want us to command fire to come down from heaven and consume them?'" Jesus told them they were wrong, and just "went on to another village" (*Luke* 9:52-57). Jesus came, not to destroy but to save. If we want to reveal ourselves as his risen body on earth, we need to cultivate within ourselves, as his disciples, the same attitude Jesus had. Faced with injustice or hostility, our immediate response should not be, "How can I fight back?" It should be life-giving: "How can I help, how can I heal this person?"

LIFE "IN THE SPIRIT"

Romans 8:8-11 makes clear that there is a radical difference between thinking and living in the way that seems most natural to us—the way people in our society seem to think, the way we grew up thinking, the way our culture conditions us to think and react—and the way Jesus thinks and acts. St. Paul calls the first way "living in the flesh," following what our physical contact with others in human society has programmed us to think and do. He calls the second way "living in the Spirit," following what our experience of the Spirit in our hearts impels us to do. Paul says, "those who are in the flesh cannot please God." They might do a lot of good things, but they can't integrally live and impact the world in the way Jesus needs them to do if they are going to be most effective in helping him establish the reign of God on earth. "But you are not in the flesh," Paul says to those who are living the life of grace and listening to Jesus as disciples. "You are in the Spirit, since the Spirit of God dwells in you."

This is the way we experience Jesus' triumph and Jesus' life in us: "If the Spirit of him who raised Jesus from the dead dwells in you, he who raised Christ from the dead will give life to your mortal bodies also through his Spirit that dwells in you." This is not just physical life: we will find that we "come alive" in faith, hope, and love and can do Christ's work in the world as his living body, enlightened and strengthened by his Spirit. Then we ourselves will be the visible proof of Jesus' resurrection, because we will be living manifestly by his Spirit as his risen body on earth.

"LAZARUS, COME OUT!"

But we have to hear his voice. And we can. **John 11:1-45** tells us that Lazarus was four days in the tomb; nevertheless, in response to the voice of Jesus he "came out," though his hands and feet were "bound with strips of cloth." If we let the words of Jesus call us forth, we too will "come out" of whatever binds us and keeps us in darkness or in the death of inertia. We will experience Christ's triumph and his "great power to redeem" through the divine life he shares with us and the action of his Spirit within us.

But for this to happen we have to *hear his words.* We need to become *disciples,* learners, and *listen* to Jesus. We need to reflect on his words and let them call us to life. His words open us to the Spirit, and the Spirit gives us life. "For with the LORD there is steadfast love, and with him is *great power to redeem.*" We have to believe this enough to dedicate ourselves to learning from him as committed students of his mind and heart.

INSIGHT

Do I live more by the "Spirit" or by the "flesh"? When have I experienced the light and power of the Spirit in me?

INITIATIVE:

Read Scripture every day—even if only for five minutes—and let it challenge the attitudes and assumptions you grew up with.

APRIL 11, 2011

The *Responsorial* (*Psalm* 23) declares all fears false except separation from God: *"Though I walk in the valley of darkness, I fear no evil; for you are at my side."*

Daniel 13:1-62 is a painful story to read today, and it raises painful issues. The villains are "elders," which in Greek is *presbyteros*, the word which became "priest" in English. In the context of our world, the men who tried to rape Susanna were priests. Worse than that, they were "judges," which makes them closer to bishops. Although Suzanna was a married woman, we cannot read this without feeling the shadow of the disgrace that Catholic priests and bishops brought upon the Church through commission, collusion, or cover-up in the recently unveiled horror of child-abuse.

The relevance and practical value of the story for us lies in the reason why Susanna was found guilty. With her unblemished reputation, the people might not have accepted the testimony of two ordinary men. But her accusers had the credibility that two bishops or cardinals would have in a Church hearing today. Any lawyer will tell you that, although justice is supposed to be blind, justice through a jury can be swayed by the prestige of the witnesses.

The child-abuse horror is a story of *clericalism*, defined as the unmerited assumption that priests and bishops are somehow more sacred and more holy than ordinary people. Priests could prey on children because the children were in awe of them as representatives of God. Parents reported abusers to the bishop because they thought priests too sacred to be handed over to the police. And they trusted—mistakenly—that the bishop would handle the matter on a higher, holier level than the government. Like the judges who accused Susanna, they were initially assumed to be beyond reproach. Hopefully, we will never make that mistake again.

We have learned a bitter lesson. In God's human-divine Church, no rank, position, function, even sacramentally bestowed, makes anyone holier or more to be trusted *a-priori* than anyone else. Our theology tells us the sacraments produce their result independently of the holiness of the minister. That also should tell us the holiness of the minister is not to be presumed without some corroborating evidence. What Jesus said of true and false prophets is also true of good and bad clerics: "You will know them by their fruits."[1]

In **John 8:1-11** Jesus shows us that it is also wrong to presume anyone is "bad," even a sinner "caught in the act" of adultery. Jesus said to the woman, "I do not condemn you." But he did condemn the action: "From now on, avoid this sin." No matter what we do, Jesus will not forsake us: *"Though I walk in the valley of darkness... you are at my side."*

[1] *Matthew* 7:15-20.

Initiative: Put aside prejudice, whether for or against any person. Speak truth.

APRIL 12, 2011

The *Responsorial* (*Psalm* 102) tells us what to say when we are just tired of following Christ: *"O Lord, hear my prayer, and let my cry come to you."*

In **Numbers 21:4-9** the people were tired of following Moses through the desert. They "complained against God" because food and drink were scarce in the desert, and what they got didn't satisfy them: "We are disgusted with this wretched food."

We may not have traveled in the desert. But if we have been disciples for very long in the true sense—"students" of God's mind and heart through reading and meditation—we know what it is to be "dry." There are times when reading God's word is like eating sawdust without salt. And times when any religious act, from devotions to Eucharist, just makes us "disgusted."

Sometimes it is not that bad. But we are just bored and tired of "putting in the time" on whatever our spiritual "fitness program" is. That is when we pass or fail to pass the test. (Actually, most of us fail it many times, but God keeps giving us retakes).

God doesn't send serpents to afflict us. He doesn't have to. Once we have begun to "seek the face of God," if we stop seeking it we feel the difference. We may not fall back into previous sins (or we may), but we will live with the sense that something is lacking in our lives. We will keep getting little bites until we either "die" by giving up entirely, or learn to turn to God: *"O Lord, hear my prayer, and let my cry come to you."*

When we know we can't persevere just by will power (although sometimes it will feel like that's all we've got), God will give us help that lets us appreciate everything we do as a gift of God.

John 8:21-30 explains that the "bronze serpent" is the symbol of Jesus on the cross. It teaches us discipleship is not just a human exercise. The *Liturgy of the Word* leads us to what we celebrate in the *Liturgy of the Eucharist*: the mystery of dying and rising in Christ.

Jesus said the problem with being Christian is: "You belong to what is below—this world. I belong to what is above." Jesus is divine; he is God. But it took his dying and rising to reveal it: "When you *lift up* the Son of Man you will come to realize that I AM."

> Just as Moses lifted up the serpent in the wilderness, so must the Son of Man be lifted up (*John* 3:14).

To be Christian is to "become Christ." We can only do this by looking to Jesus "lifted up" on the cross and letting ourselves be lifted up with him by incorporation into his body at Baptism. By this we die in him and rise to live as his own human-divine body on earth. We are *disciples* to learn how to do this.

But living as Christ can only be learned by *surrender* to letting Jesus act *with* us, in us, and *through* us. When we can do no more, we look to him in whom we are and pray, *"O Lord, hear my prayer, and let my cry come to you.* Do what I am doing *with* me, *in* me, and *through* me."

Initiative: Say the WIT prayer. Persevere in human efforts to be divine.

APRIL 13, 2011

The *Responsorial* (*Daniel* 3:52-56) affirms: *"Glory and praise forever!"*

St. Ignatius of Loyola defines "three degrees of humility"—three levels of understanding about ourselves in relationship to God. The first is:

> I so subject and humble myself as to obey the law of God in all things, so that not even were I made lord of all creation, or to save my life here on earth, would I consent to violate a commandment... that binds me under pain of mortal sin.[1]

Daniel 3:14-95 gives an example of three young men who fit that description perfectly. They were young Jews

> of the nobility, young men without any defect, handsome, intelligent and wise, quick to learn.... who were to be taught the language and literature of the Chaldeans. After three years' training they were to enter the king's service (ch.1:3-5).

Smart politics: integrating the conquered into the culture. They were made administrators in Babylon. But when the king wanted to impose religious uniformity on his kingdom, they refused. When threatened with death, they replied: "If our God, whom we serve, can save us from the white-hot furnace... may he save us! But know, O King, that even if he will not, we will not serve your god."

God did save them, but the point is, being unfaithful to God was for them simply a non-negotiable. Not even to think about. That is the first level of authentic relationship to God.

The three young men learned Chaldean culture but did not abandon their own. They remained uncompromising Jews, faithful to the Covenant. In **John 8:31-42** Jesus argues with others who claim the same thing. He had said, "If you live according to my teaching, you will truly be my disciples. You will know the truth, and the truth will set you free." They answer, "We are descendants of Abraham. Never have we been slaves to anyone." But Jesus tells them they are: "Everyone who lives in sin is the slave of sin." Might we be unfaithful without knowing it?

Many young Catholics, "intelligent and wise, quick to learn...." are selected by our system for four years of higher education, "after which they are to enter the service" of the American dream. With great rewards. They are not asked to kneel before a golden statue. But they may be required to subordinate their values to the god of gold. Or of success. Or corporate power. Or of relativistic philosophy. Or the god of No-god-at-all. In the name of an unavowed religious uniformity, "fitting in" may mean rejecting all religions as divisive. If they refuse, they will be "burned." If they accept, they may not even know they have.

Jesus gives four "if's" to help us know if we are free: "If you live according to my teaching..." "If the Son frees you" (through personal interaction with him). "If you are Abraham's children": faithful to your heritage, e.g. still going to Mass... "If God is your Father," not just your Creator and Judge. Four benchmarks.

[1] *Spiritual Exercises*, no. 165.

Initiative: Make fidelity non-negotiable. Refuse slavery. Identify false gods.

APRIL 14, 2011

The *Responsorial* (*Psalm* 105) gives one side of the picture: *"The Lord remembers his covenant forever."*

Genesis 17:3-9 is a weak promise compared to what Jesus promised those who accept his "New Covenant." To Abraham God promised human benefits: "I will render you fertile, make nations of you... give to you the land where you are now as a permanent possession." But Jesus promises us a "posterity" alive with the life of God; and the Kingdom of God as our "permanent possession" for all eternity. Beginning with Mary, who gave flesh to God himself, we will bear spiritual fruit:

> Blessed are you among women, and blessed is the fruit of your womb.

Blessed are we all. Blessed is the fruit of our lives. Like Paul, we are "in the pain of childbirth" until Christ is alive and fully formed in every person. All we help to grow in grace are our "children."

This is the fruit of *discipleship*: those who hear the word and accept it" will "bear fruit, 30, 60, 100 times over":

> I chose you... to go and bear fruit, fruit that will last....

> My Father is glorified by this, that you bear much fruit and become my disciples....

In Baptism we "died to the law" and to every human rule of life, so that "through the body of Christ" we might "belong to another, to him who has been raised from the dead in order that we may bear fruit for God." This comes through absorption in:

the word of the truth, the gospel that has come to you. Just as it is bearing fruit and growing in the whole world, so it has been bearing fruit among yourselves from the day you heard it and truly comprehended the grace of God.[1]

That is just one side of the picture: "On your part," God adds, "you must keep my covenant throughout the ages." Christian life is a commitment.

In **John 8:51-59** Jesus claims to be divine: "I solemnly declare it: before Abraham came to be, I AM." This is the translation of YAHWEH, the self-description God gave when Moses asked him to reveal his "name."[2]

As Christ's disciples, we study, not just words, but the words of the Word. This makes a difference in our commitment.

We made a covenant at Baptism with the Word of God. It was at the same time a covenant with the words of God: we are committed to seek understanding of the Word through his words. This is a "constitutive element" of being a Christian. To "love the Lord our God with all our heart, and with all our soul, and with all our mind," we have to use our minds to know him. St. Augustine said, "We cannot love what we do not know." The conclusion is obvious. We are committed by our baptismal covenant to be "students of the word," disciples of the Word expressing himself in words. *"The Lord remembers his covenant forever."* The question is, "Do we?"

[1]*Luke* 1:42; *Galatians* 4:19; *Mark* 4:20; *John* 15·8, 16; *Romans* 7:4; *Colossians* 1:5 6.
[2]*Exodus* 3:14; see *Isaiah* 41:4-14 and 43:1-13; *John* 4:26; 6:20; 8:24-28; 13:19; 18:5-8. "I am he" can also be translated, "I am.

Initiative: Face the Word. Commit to discovering him in his words.

APRIL 15, 2011

The *Responsorial* (*Psalm* 18) is a reminder we never stop feeling the need for: "*In my distress I called upon the Lord and he heard my voice.*"

Jeremiah 20:10-13 shows us what Jesus predicted for his disciples:

"Terror on every side! Denounce! Let us denounce him." Those who were my friends are on the watch for any misstep of mine.

Jesus said, "Do you think that I have come to bring peace to the earth? No, I tell you, but rather division!"

See, I am sending you out like sheep into the midst of wolves... Beware of them.... Brother will betray brother to death, and a father his child.... You will be hated by all because of my name.

It takes courage to study God's word. We may get insights we don't want—about ourselves, others, friends, and family, the Church, the world we live in. (That first came out as a typo: "the world we lie in." Also true). Once we see the truth, what do we do with it? Put it under a bushel basket? Speak it? Live it out? The last two can get us in trouble. But Jesus calls this peace!

I have said this to you, so that in me you may have peace. In the world you face persecution. But take courage; I have conquered the world![1]

The assurance of victory gives peace even in the midst of conflict. "*In my distress I called upon the Lord and he heard my voice*"—and answered, "Peace!"

John 10:31-42 is all about Jesus' identity. His enemies were stoning him because "you who are only a man are making yourself God."

If we are honest in professing our faith, the same can be said of us. We say we are the actual, physical body of Christ, not just God's creatures but his true children. His own divine life is in us, because we are *filii in Filio*, "sons and daughters *in the Son*." Each of us says with St. Paul, "It is no longer I who live, but it is Christ who lives in me." By Baptism we have "*become Christ*."

And we claim that this groping, sinful "pilgrim Church" we are is uniquely the "one true Church" of Jesus Christ! While all Christian assemblies have something of his Church in them, we alone have all that is required to be the full Church Jesus founded. Does that make us popular?[2]

Jesus said, "If I do not perform my Father's works, put no faith in me." We as a Church may hesitate to suggest that, but people will do it anyway. If the "fruit of the Spirit" is not visible in us; if we don't obviously love God and all our neighbors; read and reflect on God's word as *disciples*; live a lifestyle different from our culture as *prophets*; celebrate liturgy with enthusiasm and nurture one another as *priests*; care for the poor and work to establish the reign of God's justice and peace on earth as *stewards* of his kingship, no proofs from Scripture or theology will convince anyone that we actually are the living body of Jesus Christ on earth.

[1] *Luke* 12:51; *Matthew* 10:16-22; *John* 16:33. See *John* 7:40-43; 15:18-20.
[2] See *Romans* 12:1-5; *Galatians* 2:20; *Catechism of the Catholic Church*, nos. 795, 460.

Initiative: Have the courage to read, reflect, speak, and do. *Be Christ* visibly.

APRIL 16, 2011

The *Responsorial* (from *Jeremiah* 31:10-13) is a promise for all time: *"The Lord will guard us as a shepherd guards his flock."*

In **Ezekiel 37:21-28** God is promising to restore unity to his People by uniting the tribes again as they were under King David.[1] But it was under the kingship of the promised "Son of David" that true unity would be restored; not just to Israel, but to the human race. The "miracle of tongues" at Pentecost was a sign and preview of this; when God reversed the Tower of Babel by letting people present "from every nation under heaven" understand the apostles speaking the "language of the Spirit."[2]

Paul announced God's "plan for the fullness of time, to gather up all things in Christ, things in heaven and things on earth." Paul was sent to the Gentiles so that through him Christ "might create in himself one new humanity in place of the two, thus making peace":

> So then you are no longer strangers and aliens, but citizens with the saints and members of the household of God... with Christ Jesus himself as the cornerstone... in whom you also are built together spiritually into a dwelling place for God.[3]

This unity was broken by the schism between Catholics of East and West, and by the Protestant Reformation. We can never rest until unity is restored. What is holding it back?

It is an axiom in most organizations that "the buck stops" at the top. John Paul II may have been thinking this when he said that if his way of "exercising the primacy" was keeping the Eastern Rites separated, he would change it. "This is an immense task, which we cannot refuse and which I cannot carry out by myself." He asked for "a patient and fraternal dialogue... in which, leaving useless controversies behind, we could listen to one another, keeping before us only the will of Christ for his Church and allowing ourselves to be deeply moved by his plea 'that they may all be one....'"[4]

This sets a principle for all renewal in the Church. The authorities—bishops, pastors, and lay professionals in charge of various ministries—have more power than anyone to bring about reforms, but without the committed participation of everyone else, lay and cleric, it will be "too little, too late."

John 11:45-57 tells us that when the high priest said, "It is better to have one man die than the whole nation destroyed," he unknowingly "prophesied that Jesus would die for the nation... and to gather into one all the dispersed children of God."

So what are you willing to do to bring about unity? In your home? Parish? School? Workplace? With other Christians? With Muslims? Other non-Christians? The non-churched? What would you have to "die" to? If we are as willing as Jesus was, then *"the Lord will guard us as a shepherd guards his flock."*

[1] *2Samuel* 5:1-3.
[2] *Acts* 2:12.
[3] *Ephesians* 1:9-10; 2:13-22.
[4] See the encyclical *Ut Unum Sint*, nos. 95-96.

Initiative: Strive for unity. Believe in each one's grace. Hope for change. Love.

FOR REFLECTION AND DISCUSSION: LENT WEEK FIVE

We are the risen body of Jesus. In and through us he is winning the battle today.

Invitation: Live by the Spirit. Dedicate yourself to *listen* to Jesus as a *disciple* of his mind and heart. Let his words open you to the Spirit, and let the Spirit give you life.

Ask yourself in prayer and others in discussion, for each statement below: Do you see this in the Scripture reading? What response does it invite?

Sunday: We know Jesus is triumphing, not from what we see happening in the world around us, but from what we see happening within ourselves.

Faced with injustice or hostility, our immediate response should not be, "How can I fight back?" It should be life-giving: "How can I help, how can I heal this person?"

Monday: The child-abuse horror is a story of *clericalism*, defined as the unmerited assumption that priests and bishops are more sacred than laypersons.

In God's human-divine Church, no rank, position, function, even sacramentally bestowed, makes anyone holier or more to be trusted *a-priori* than anyone else.

Tuesday: "Dryness" teaches us that discipleship is not just human discipline and will-power but a gift of God.

Living as Christ can only be learned by *surrender* to letting Jesus act *with* us, in us, and *through* us.

Wednesday: When being unfaithful to God is for us simply a non-negotiable, we have reached the first level of proper relationship to God.

Jesus gives four benchmarks of spiritual freedom: • living by Christ's teaching; • being free through personal interaction with Christ; • being faithful to our heritage (e.g. still going to Mass); • knowing God as Father, not just Creator and Judge.

Thursday: Jesus promises us more than God promised Abraham: 1. a "posterity" of people to whom we have communicated the divine life of God; and 2. the Kingdom of God as our "permanent possession" for all eternity.

Friday: It takes courage to study God's word. But the assurance of victory gives peace even in the midst of conflict.

Saturday: Each of us must be willing to "die" to whatever in us is an obstacle to unity—in our home, parish, workplace, with other Christians and non-Christians.

Decisions:

Say the WIT prayer. Persevere in human efforts to stay conscious of being divine.

Have the courage to read, reflect, speak, and do. *Be Christ* visibly.

Promote unity. Believe in each one's grace. Hope for change. Live in love.

April 17, 2011
PALM SUNDAY OF THE LORD'S PASSION
Conversion to Unconditional Discipleship

INVENTORY

Do I ever grow weary of praying? Do I sometimes feel it is useless, that nothing ever comes of it? That God just doesn't care about me? Did Jesus feel this?

INPUT

The *Responsorial* (*Psalm 22*) is the verse Jesus quoted on the cross: *"My God, my God, why have you abandoned me?"* It is a song of trust and triumph: "In you our ancestors trusted... and were not put to shame... For dominion belongs to the LORD, and he rules over the nations." Jesus was calling up this Psalm to counter the abandonment he felt in his heart. This pinpoints the theme of all the readings.

In the *Opening Prayer* we focus on Jesus as a "model of humility" because he subjected himself to human weakness like ours. We ask God to "help us bear witness to you" by trusting in God's power when our weakness crushes us.

EVERY MORNING:

Isaiah 50:4-7 is a declaration of perseverance based on trust. Isaiah recognizes that he is called to discipleship because he is sent to teach: "The Lord GOD has given me the tongue of a teacher, that I may know how to sustain the weary with a word."

We are all called to teach. Jesus said to his disciples, "You are the light of the world.... No one after lighting a lamp puts it under a bushel basket, but on a lamp stand.... Let your light shine before others" (*Matthew 5:14-16*).

To do this we must be committed to persevering discipleship, to persistent reading and reflection on the Scriptures, and to open-minded discussion of Christ's teaching. Isaiah testifies to his own faithfulness to discipleship: *"Morning after morning* he wakens my ear to *listen"*—as a student.

WHAT JESUS FELT:

Philippians 2:6-11 tells us Jesus experienced the same human difficulties we do. We may think that because Jesus was God, prayer always came easy to him; that he never experienced temptations to doubt; that nothing in him ever resisted the Father's will.

But this isn't true. In his agony in the garden (*Matthew 26:37-46*) Jesus felt "deeply grieved"—so much so that on the emotional level he was ready to call off his whole passion: "My Father, if it is possible, let this cup pass from me!" His feelings were intensely opposed to what God wanted him to do. But feelings are not the measure of anyone's faith, hope, or love—neither in Jesus nor in us. In the garden Jesus did not *feel* any desire to die for us. But on the level that really counts, the level of *will and free choice*, he was firm: "Yet not what I want but what you want."

When Jesus became human he became really human, with no privileges. "Though he was in the form of God, he did not regard equality with God as something to be exploited, but emptied himself," being born just as human as we are, with all the weaknesses that belong to being human, sin excepted. "For we do not have a high priest who is unable to sympathize with our weaknesses, but we have one who in every respect has been tested as we are, yet without sin" (*Hebrews* 4:15).

This same Jesus, by taking our bodies to be his own, has also taken on our weakness—and given us his strength. That is the rock-bottom source of our confidence.

TRIUMPH BY DEFEAT:

Today's Mass is called both "Passion Sunday" and "Palm Sunday," because it begins with a procession in which we carry palms. We read two Gospels: the *Passion* (**Matthew 26:4 to 27:66**) and one for the procession (**Matthew 21:1-11**), when we ritually celebrate Jesus' entrance into Jerusalem as the crowd that accompanied him spread their cloaks on the road, and cut branches from the trees and spread them on the road, shouting, "Hosanna to the Son of David! Blessed is the one who comes in the name of the Lord!"

This scene gives a key to understanding Christ's passion and all of his work in the Church since then: *the strategy of God is that Jesus wins by losing.* He enters Jerusalem in triumph to die. His defeat and death on the cross were his victory over sin and death. And in the world today, when the Church seems most weak and defeated, that is when God is able to do the best work in us. A poor and humiliated Church is a healthy Church.

In our personal lives, when we feel the least faith, hope, and love, that is precisely when we may be acting most purely out of nothing but faith, hope, and love. When our feelings give us no support, but we are still trying to do what we committed ourselves to do, we know we are persevering by the pure grace of God. That is the most unambiguous experience of grace. It is the ultimate verification of conversion. And it is the touchstone of dedicated discipleship. When our feelings are crying out, "My God, why have you abandoned me?" but we have not abandoned him, that is when we know most surely God is near.

Jesus said, "The disciple is not greater than the teacher" (*Matthew* 10:24). If we are showing up as disciples, Jesus is showing up as Teacher, whether we feel him there or not.

INSIGHT

In my ordinary life, when have I gone against my feelings to persevere in something I decided to do? Were the results good? Can I do the same with prayer?

INITIATIVE:

Decide what you will do to be a disciple—how much time you will commit to reading, reflecting, and other learning experiences—and determine to persevere.

April 18, 2011

The *Responsorial* (*Psalm* 27) invites us to find life through light: *"The Lord is my light and my salvation."*

Isaiah 42:1-7 is the first *"Song of the Servant of Yahweh,"* whom God calls "my chosen one with whom I am well pleased." But the description is valid for anyone who would do the work of God. As *disciples* we ponder the characteristics of the person God chooses for his work, to whom he says, "On you I have put my spirit."

- One who will "bring forth justice";
- "not shouting out... in the streets";[1]
- who "will not break the crushed reed";
- who "will not grow faint" before "establishing fair judgment on earth";
- for whose teaching the ends of the earth are "waiting."

The God who chooses this kind of person is the exultant Creator who "spreads out the heavens," and "gives breath and spirit to people."

His desire is clear: "I called you for the victory of justice, as a light for the nations, to open the eyes of the blind, and bring out prisoners who live in darkness." He wants life, light, freedom.

God "grasped by the hand" and "formed" his servant. Intimacy. Guidance. Do these points give something to think about?

John 12:1-11 shows us a contrast. First there is Mary, who like the exultant, profligate Creator in Isaiah, pours out on Jesus' feet a pound of perfume so expensive it would take a laborer's whole yearly wage to buy it. Crazy! Extravagant. Passionate. Like God!

Judas makes the called-for objection: "We could have sold it! And given the money to the poor!" If he himself were giving extravagantly to the poor, we could accept that. But what he really shows is a mind that can't see beyond dollars-and-cents to passionate love. Even if he hadn't been stealing he would have been horrified. He had a small heart. Passion doesn't count pennies. Or stop to count anything!

St. Ignatius says we make more spiritual progress through one really generous act than ten run-of-the-mill sacrifices. Why? Because we get a taste of what God is like. We get it by treating God like God, which, paradoxically, is the way to experience how God treats us—with boundless love and generosity.

It figures: God is "in-finite" (without *fines*, the Latin for boundaries). If we try to respond to God without boundaries, we get a hint of what it is like not to have any. St. Ignatius' prayer was:

Dearest Lord, teach me to be generous.
To serve you as you deserve.
To give and not to count the cost.
To fight and not to heed the wounds.
To toil and not to seek for rest.
To labor and not ask for reward—
Save that of knowing I am doing your will.

We could do worse. The core of both these readings is the picture of a God who exults in giving life and being, and invites us to be the same. *"The Lord is my light and my salvation."*

[1] He "accomplishes his mission modestly and quietly, not whipping people into conformity but transforming them interiorly." *Jerome Biblical Commentary, 1968.*

Initiative: Do something extravagant: for someone else or for yourself. Feel God.

TUESDAY HOLY WEEK

APRIL 19, 2011

The *Responsorial* (*Psalm* 71) is a reflex response: *"I will sing of your salvation."*

Isaiah 49:1-6 is the beginning of the second *Song of the Servant*. These songs

> portray the ideal Servant of God, the perfect Israelite, whose consecration to the divine will, even in the midst of overwhelming suffering, 'takes away the sins of many.'

The Servant's identity is complex:

> The Servant is "Israel, alive in all of her great leaders and intercessors.... But the collective interpretation leads to an individual Servant of supreme holiness, greater than any single Israelite of the past.... It was Jesus who clearly identified himself as the Servant.... The Servant is both a collective personality and an individual messiah."[1]

For practical purposes we can apply what is said about the Servant to Jesus, to Israel, to the Church, and to ourselves. Individually and collectively, we are all engaged in his mission, and we experience what he experiences in fulfilling it. Four points to keep in mind:

• The Servant knows he was chosen "from my mother's womb." So do we—at least from the womb of Baptism. So did Jesus. But he was tempted to doubt it, as we are.[2]

• He feels he has "toiled in vain and for nothing." So did Jesus, who on the cross felt failure and abandonment. So do we.

• He knows his "reward is with the Lord." So did Jesus. In his human consciousness he did not know on the cross that he would rise from the dead. But like Abraham sacrificing Isaac, he believed, "hoping against hope," that he was inexplicably saving the world and entering into his glory. We sometimes need to do the same.[3]

• In response to his discouragement, God extends his mission beyond Israel to include the whole earth: "I will make you a light to the nations, that my salvation may reach to the ends of the earth." When the pot is empty, throw a party! After Good Friday comes Pentecost. *"I will sing of your salvation."*

John 13:21-38 shows us Jesus aware of betrayal and denial by two of his closest followers, and his response is to say, "Now is the Son of Man glorified, and God is glorified in him!" He knew things were out of his hands. He was to be delivered up. He had no human support. But he knew the Scriptural principle: In the absence of the human the divine is revealed. The Virgin Birth: the absence of a human father revealed the fatherhood of God. Sending his disciples without resources to show they relied on God.[4] His present situation: the absence of all human support meant he was in the hands of God. If God was allowing his total abasement, God must be glorifying him. There was nothing more to do but surrender in joy: "Father, into your hands I commend my spirit." *"I will sing of your salvation."*

---

[1]*Jerome Biblical Commentary, 1968.*
[2]See his temptations, beginning with "If..." *Matthew* 4:1-11; 27:39-46.
[3]*Romans* 4:18; *John* 12:23-28.
[4]*Matthew* 10:9-10.

Initiative: Find life in death, hope in despair, light in darkness, love in abandonment, power in weakness. In the absence of the human, rejoice in God.

APRIL 20, 2011

The *Responsorial* (read all of *Psalm* 69) is the constant prayer of the servants of God: *"Lord, in your great love, answer me."*

Isaiah 50:4-9 is the third *Song of the Servant*. The Servant neither depends on human support nor fears human opposition. His confidence is in God.

• God has equipped him: "The Lord God has given me a well-trained tongue." Think of how God has equipped us in the Church. But for our "tongue" to serve, it must be "trained" through *use* of "word and sacrament."

• Training is ongoing: "Morning after morning he opens my ear that I may hear." The Servant is a continuing *disciple*. He listens. Daily. "The Servant must first be a disciple, prayerfully receiving God's word, before he can presume to teach others."[1]

• He accepts persecution and suffering without resentment: "I have not rebelled, have not turned back. I gave my back to those who beat me...." The "way of the cross" is to endure evil and *love back*.

• He relies on God for strength and victory: "The Lord God is my help, therefore I am not disgraced."

• This is the source of his courage and perseverance. Nothing is going to turn him aside from his mission: "I have set my face like flint, knowing that I shall not be put to shame." "See, the Lord God is my help."

Mathew 26:14-25 shows us another contrast. Judas looks ahead and sees that Jesus is going to go down. So he takes care of himself. He takes his stakes out of the pot and invests in the future. He goes over to the enemy, the "chief priests," and asks, "What will you give me if I hand him over to you?"

By contrast, when the other disciples look ahead, they go to Jesus: "Where do you wish us to prepare the Passover supper for you?" They are with him and have cast in their lot with him. They trust in whatever he says.

Jesus answers as he did when they asked him how to feed the crowd following him in the wilderness. Then he told them to call on the community, ask them to share. "How many loaves have you? Go and see." They found a boy with "five barley loaves and two fish."

Now he says, "Go to this man in the city..."—obviously a believer—"...and tell him, 'the Teacher says my appointed time draws near. I am to celebrate the Passover with my disciples in your house.'" Jesus knows he will share.

"When it grew dark, he reclined at table with the Twelve"—soon to be eleven. As night approached, all they had was themselves and God. It was enough.

Except for Judas. After receiving the "bread" from Jesus' hand, he "immediately went out." Then, John wrote, "It was night."[2]

[1] *Jerome Biblical Commentary*, 1968.
[2] *Mark* 6:38; *John* 6:9; 13;26-30.

Initiative: In any need, pray *"Lord, in your great love, answer me."*

FOR REFLECTION AND DISCUSSION: HOLY WEEK

Note: *Holy Thursday, Good Friday, the Holy Saturday Easter Vigil, and Easter Sunday are all one extended celebration of Easter called the "Easter Triduum" (three days from Thursday evening to Sunday evening). So we end these reflections on the Lenten season with Wednesday and we will begin the Easter season with reflections on Holy Thursday.*

Reading God's word lets us understand what we celebrate. Celebration makes what is in the word real and active in our lives. Liturgy unites light to life and us to one another in the "communion of the Holy Spirit."

Invitation: When feelings give no support, persevere. When we feel the least faith, hope, and love, we may be acting most purely out of nothing but faith, hope, and love.

Ask yourself in prayer and others in discussion, for each statement below: Do you see this in the Scripture reading? What response does it invite?

Sunday: Jesus wins by losing. He enters Jerusalem in triumph to die. His defeat and death were his victory. When the Church seems most weak and defeated, God is able to do his best work in us. A poor and humiliated Church is a healthy Church.

In his agony in the garden Jesus did not *feel* any desire to die for us. But on the level of *will and free choice*, he was firm. Feelings are not the measure.

Monday: God is "in-finite." If we try to respond to him without boundaries, we get a hint of what it is like not to have any.

Tuesday: We are like Jesus because: • We know we were chosen, though we are tempted to doubt it; • We sometimes feel we have "toiled in vain and for nothing"; • We know our "reward is with the Lord"; • In response to our discouragement, God tells us to extend our mission.

A Scriptural principle is: In the absence of the human the divine is revealed. The absence of all human support tells us we are in the hands of God.

Wednesday: Like the "Servant of Yahweh": • We neither depend on human support nor fear human opposition. • We are "equipped" but must be "trained" through *use* of "word and sacrament." • We are continuing *disciples*; our training is ongoing. • We endure evil and *love back*. • We rely on God for strength and victory.

Decisions:

Decide what you will do to be a disciple. How much time will you commit to reading, reflecting, and other learning experiences—determined to persevere?

Find life in death, hope in despair, light in darkness, love in abandonment, power in weakness. In the absence of the human, rejoice in God.